Cram101 Textbook Outlines to accompany:

Pathophysiology - Biology Basis for Disease in Adults and Children

Kathryn L. McCance, 5th Edition

A Cram101 Inc. publication (c) 2010.

PRACTICE EXAMS.

Get all of the self-teaching practice exams for each chapter of this textbook at **www.Cram101.com** and ace the tests. Here is an example:

Chapter 1

Pathophysiology - Biology Basis for Disease in Adults and Children
Kathryn L. McCance, 5th Edition,
All Material Written and Prepared by Cram101

I WANT A BETTER GRADE.

Items 1 - 50 of 100.

1   A _____ is any malignant cancer that arises from epithelial cells. _____ s invade surrounding tissues and organs and may metastasize, or spread, to lymph nodes and other sites.

⊙ Carcinoma   ⊙ Calamine
⊙ Calcium benzoate   ⊙ Calcium hypochlorite

2   _____ are cellular organs possessed by Apicomplexa protozoans. They are specialized secretory organelles important for gliding motility and host cell invasion.

Subdomains/Superkingdoms

⊙ Micronemes   ⊙ Macbecin
⊙ Macrolide   ⊙ Madonna Swan

3   _____ is a class of diseases in which a group of cells display uncontrolled growth (division beyond the normal limits), invasion

---

You get a 50% discount for the online exams. Go to **Cram101.com**, click Sign Up at the top of the screen, and enter DK73DW7942 in the promo code box on the registration screen. Access to Cram101.com is $4.95 per month, cancel at any time.

With Cram101.com online, you also have access to extensive reference material.

You will nail those essays and papers. Here is an example from a Cram101 Biology text:

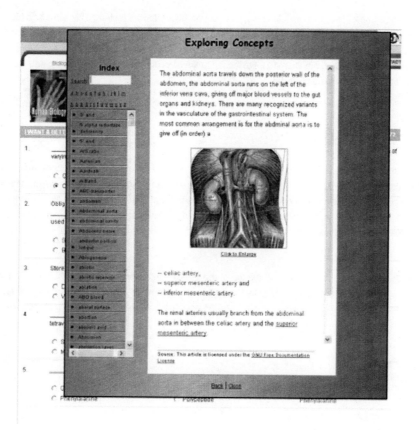

Visit **www.Cram101.com**, click Sign Up at the top of the screen, and enter DK73DW7942 in the promo code box on the registration screen. Access to www.Cram101.com is normally $9.95 per month, but because you have purchased this book, your access fee is only $4.95 per month, cancel at any time. Sign up and stop highlighting textbooks forever.

Learning System

Cram101 Textbook Outlines is a learning system. The notes in this book are the highlights of your textbook, you will never have to highlight a book again.

How to use this book. Take this book to class, it is your notebook for the lecture. The notes and highlights on the left hand side of the pages follow the outline and order of the textbook. All you have to do is follow along while your instructor presents the lecture. Circle the items emphasized in class and add other important information on the right side. With Cram101 Textbook Outlines you'll spend less time writing and more time listening. Learning becomes more efficient.

Cram101.com Online

Increase your studying efficiency by using Cram101.com's practice tests and online reference material. It is the perfect complement to Cram101 Textbook Outlines. Use self-teaching matching tests or simulate in-class testing with comprehensive multiple choice tests, or simply use Cram's true and false tests for quick review. Cram101.com even allows you to enter your in-class notes for an integrated studying format combining the textbook notes with your class notes.

Visit **www.Cram101.com**, click Sign Up at the top of the screen, and enter **DK73DW7942** in the promo code box on the registration screen. Access to www.Cram101.com is normally $9.95 per month, but because you have purchased this book, your access fee is only $4.95 per month. Sign up and stop highlighting textbooks forever.

Pathophysiology - Biology Basis for Disease in Adults and Children
Kathryn L. McCance, 5th

CONTENTS

Pathophysiology - Biology Basis for Disease in Adults and Children
Kathryn L. McCance, 5th

CONTENTS (continued)

Carcinoma	A Carcinoma is any malignant cancer that arises from epithelial cells. Carcinoma s invade surrounding tissues and organs and may metastasize, or spread, to lymph nodes and other sites.

Micronemes		Micronemes are cellular organs possessed by Apicomplexa protozoans. They are specialized secretory organelles important for gliding motility and host cell invasion.

Subdomains/Superkingdoms

Cancer	Cancer is a class of diseases in which a group of cells display uncontrolled growth (division beyond the normal limits), invasion (intrusion on and destruction of adjacent tissues), and sometimes metastasis (spread to other locations in the body via lymph or blood.) These three malignant properties of cancers differentiate them from benign tumors, which are self-limited, and do not invade or metastasize. Most cancers form a tumor but some, like leukemia, do not.
Electrolyte	An Electrolyte is any substance containing free ions that behaves as an electrically conductive medium. Because they generally consist of ions in solution, Electrolyte s are also known as ionic solutions, but molten Electrolyte s and solid Electrolyte s are also possible. Electrolyte s commonly exist as solutions of acids, bases or salts.
Pemphigus	Pemphigus is a rare group of autoimmune blistering diseases that affect the skin and mucous membranes. In Pemphigus, autoantibodies form against desmoglein. Desmoglein forms the "glue" that attaches adjacent epidermal cells via attachment points called desmosomes.
Neoplasm	Neoplasm is an abnormal mass of tissue as a result of neoplasia. Neoplasia is the abnormal proliferation of cells. The growth of this clone of cells exceeds, and is uncoordinated with, that of the normal tissues around it.

Fibroepithelial neoplasms	Fibroepithelial neoplasms are biphasic tumors. This means they consist of epithelial tissue, and stromal or mesenchymal tissue. They may be benign or malignant.
Hyperplasia	Hyperplasia is a general term referring to the proliferation of cells within an organ or tissue beyond that which is ordinarily seen (e.g. constantly dividing cells.) Hyperplasia may result in the gross enlargement of an organ, the formation of a benign tumor, or may be visible only under a microscope. Hyperplasia is different from hypertrophy in that the adaptive cell change in hypertrophy is by increased cellular size only, whereas in Hyperplasia it is by increased cellular number.
Seizure	An epileptic Seizure is a transient symptom of excessive or synchronous neuronal activity in the brain. It can manifest as an alteration in mental state, tonic or clonic movements, convulsions, and various other psychic symptoms (such as déjà vu or jamais vu.) The medical syndrome of recurrent, unprovoked Seizure s is termed epilepsy, but Seizure s can occur in people who do not have epilepsy.

Atrophy	Atrophy is the partial or complete wasting away of a part of the body. Causes of Atrophy include poor nourishment, poor circulation, loss of hormonal support, loss of nerve supply to the target organ, disuse or lack of exercise or disease intrinsic to the tissue itself. Hormonal and nerve inputs that maintain an organ or body part are referred to as trophic.
Hypertrophy	Hypertrophy is the increase in the volume of an organ or tissue due to the enlargement of its component cells. It should be distinguished from hyperplasia, in which the cells remain approximately the same size but increase in number. Although Hypertrophy and hyperplasia are two distinct process, they frequently occur together, such as in the case of the hormonally-induced proliferation and enlargement of the cells of the uterus during pregnancy.
Dysplasia	Dysplasia is a term used in pathology to refer to an abnormality in maturation of cells within a tissue. This generally consists of an expansion of immature cells, with a corresponding decrease in the number and location of mature cells. Dysplasia is often indicative of an early neoplastic process.
Metaplasia	Metaplasia is the reversible replacement of one differentiated cell type with another mature differentiated cell type. The change from one type of cell to another is generally caused by some sort of abnormal stimulus. In simplistic terms, it is as if the original cells are not robust enough to withstand the new environment, and so they change into another type more suited to the new environment.
Hyperplasia	Hyperplasia is a general term referring to the proliferation of cells within an organ or tissue beyond that which is ordinarily seen (e.g. constantly dividing cells.) Hyperplasia may result in the gross enlargement of an organ, the formation of a benign tumor, or may be visible only under a microscope. Hyperplasia is different from hypertrophy in that the adaptive cell change in hypertrophy is by increased cellular size only, whereas in Hyperplasia it is by increased cellular number.
Pathophysiology	Pathophysiology is the study of the changes of normal mechanical, physical, and biochemical functions, either caused by a disease, or resulting from an abnormal syndrome. More formally, it is the branch of medicine which deals with any disturbances of body functions, caused by disease or prodromal symptoms. An alternate definition is "the study of the biological and physical manifestations of disease as they correlate with the underlying abnormalities and physiological disturbances." The study of pathology and the study of Pathophysiology often involves substantial overlap in diseases and processes, but pathology emphasizes direct observations, while Pathophysiology emphasizes quantifiable measurements.
Oxidative stress	Oxidative stress is caused by an imbalance between the production of reactive oxygen and a biological system"s ability to readily detoxify the reactive intermediates or easily repair the resulting damage. All forms of life maintain a reducing environment within their cells. This reducing environment is preserved by enzymes that maintain the reduced state through a constant input of metabolic energy.
Fibroepithelial neoplasms	Fibroepithelial neoplasms are biphasic tumors. This means they consist of epithelial tissue, and stromal or mesenchymal tissue. They may be benign or malignant.

FISH	FISH (fluorescence in situ hybridization) is a cytogenetic technique used to detect and localize the presence or absence of specific DNA sequences on chromosomes. FISH uses fluorescent probes that bind to only those parts of the chromosome with which they show a high degree of sequence similarity. Fluorescence microscopy can be used to find out where the fluorescent probe bound to the chromosomes.
Hematoma	A Hematoma is a collection of blood outside the blood vessels, generally the result of hemorrhage internal bleeding. It is not to be confused with hemangioma which is an abnormal build up of blood vessels in the skin or internal organs. Hematoma - from Greek αῖμα, haima, blood + τωμα, t-oma, indicating an abnormality.
Abrasion	Abrasion is the loss of tooth structure by mechanical forces from a foreign element. If this force begins at the cementoenamel junction, then progression of tooth loss can be rapid since enamel is very thin in this region of the tooth. Once past the enamel, Abrasion quickly destroys the softer dentin and cementum structures.
Stroke	A Stroke is the rapidly developing loss of brain function(s) due to disturbance in the blood supply to the brain. This can be due to ischemia (lack of blood supply) caused by thrombosis or embolism or due to a hemorrhage. As a result, the affected area of the brain is unable to function, leading to inability to move one or more limbs on one side of the body, inability to understand or formulate speech, or inability to see one side of the visual field.
Cancer	Cancer is a class of diseases in which a group of cells display uncontrolled growth (division beyond the normal limits), invasion (intrusion on and destruction of adjacent tissues), and sometimes metastasis (spread to other locations in the body via lymph or blood.) These three malignant properties of cancers differentiate them from benign tumors, which are self-limited, and do not invade or metastasize. Most cancers form a tumor but some, like leukemia, do not.
Steatosis	In cellular pathology, Steatosis is the process describing the abnormal retention of lipids within a cell. It reflects an impairment of the normal processes of synthesis and elimination of triglyceride fat. Excess lipid accumulates in vesicles that displace the cytoplasm.
Fatty liver	Fatty liver steatorrhoeic hepatosis is a reversible condition where large vacuoles of triglyceride fat accumulate in liver cells via the process of steatosis. Despite having multiple causes, Fatty liver can be considered a single disease that occurs worldwide in those with excessive alcohol intake and those who are obese The condition is also associated with other diseases that influence fat metabolism.
Russell bodies	Russell bodies are eosinophilic, large, homogenous immunoglobulin-containing inclusions usually found in a plasma cell undergoing excessive synthesis of immunoglobulin; the russell body is characteristic of the distended Endoplasmic Reticulum. This is one cell variation found in Multiple Myeloma.

They are named for William Russell.

Transferrin	Transferrin is a blood plasma protein for iron ion delivery that, in humans, is encoded by the TF gene. Transferrin is a glycoprotein that binds iron very tightly but reversibly. Although iron bound to Transferrin is less than 0.1% (4 mg) of the total body iron, it is the most important iron pool, with the highest rate of turnover (25 mg/24 h.)
Bilirubin	Bilirubin is the yellow breakdown product of normal heme catabolism. Heme is found in hemoglobin, a principal component of red blood cells. Bilirubin is excreted in bile, and its levels are elevated in certain diseases.
Dystrophic calcification	Dystrophic calcification is the calcification occurring in degenerated or necrotic tissue, as in hyalinized scars, degenerated foci in leiomyomas, and caseous nodules.(A systemic mineral imbalance would elevate calcium levels in the blood and all tissues: metastatic calcification.) This occurs as a reaction to tissue damage, including as a consequence of medical device implantation.
Primary	In medicine, the reporting of symptoms by a patient may have significant psychological motivators. Psychologists sometimes categorize these motivators into primary or secondary gain. primary gain is internally good; motivationally.
Caseous necrosis	Caseous necrosis describes a form of biological tissue death, caseous meaning it has a cheese-like appearance. The dead tissue appears as a soft and white proteinaceous dead cell mass. Frequently, Caseous necrosis is associated with tuberculosis (TB.)
Granuloma	Granuloma is a medical term for a ball-like collection of immune cells which forms when the immune system attempts to wall off substances that it perceives as foreign but is unable to eliminate. Such substances include infectious organisms such as bacteria and fungi as well as other materials such as keratin, suture fragments and vegetable particles. A Granuloma is therefore a special type of inflammatory reaction that can occur in a wide variety of diseases, both infectious and non-infectious.
Liquefactive necrosis	Liquefactive necrosis is a type of necrosis which is characteristic of focal bacterial or fungal infections. In Liquefactive necrosis, the affected cell is completely digested by hydrolytic enzymes, resulting in a soft, circumscribed lesion consisting of pus and the fluid remains of necrotic tissue. After the removal of cell debris by white blood cells, a fluid filled space is left.

Electrolyte

An Electrolyte is any substance containing free ions that behaves as an electrically conductive medium. Because they generally consist of ions in solution, Electrolyte s are also known as ionic solutions, but molten Electrolyte s and solid Electrolyte s are also possible.

Electrolyte s commonly exist as solutions of acids, bases or salts.

Neoplasm

Neoplasm is an abnormal mass of tissue as a result of neoplasia. Neoplasia is the abnormal proliferation of cells. The growth of this clone of cells exceeds, and is uncoordinated with, that of the normal tissues around it.

Gingivitis

Gingivitis around the teeth is a general term for gingival diseases affecting the gingiva As generally used, the term Gingivitis refers to gingival inflammation induced by bacterial biofilms adherent to tooth surfaces.

Gingivitis can be defined as inflammation of the gingival tissue without loss of tooth attachment

Pathophysiology

Pathophysiology is the study of the changes of normal mechanical, physical, and biochemical functions, either caused by a disease, or resulting from an abnormal syndrome. More formally, it is the branch of medicine which deals with any disturbances of body functions, caused by disease or prodromal symptoms.

An alternate definition is "the study of the biological and physical manifestations of disease as they correlate with the underlying abnormalities and physiological disturbances."

The study of pathology and the study of Pathophysiology often involves substantial overlap in diseases and processes, but pathology emphasizes direct observations, while Pathophysiology emphasizes quantifiable measurements.

Infarction

In medicine, an Infarction is the process of tissue death (necrosis) caused by blockage of the tissue"s blood supply. The supplying artery may be blocked by an obstruction (e.g. an embolus, thrombus, or atherosclerotic plaque), may be mechanically compressed (e.g. tumor, volvulus, or hernia), ruptured by trauma (e.g. atherosclerosis or vasculitides), or vasoconstricted (e.g. cocaine vasoconstriction leading to myocardial Infarction)

Infarction s are commonly associated with hypertension or atherosclerosis.

Atypia	Atypia is a clinical term for abnormality in a cell. The term is medical jargon for an atypical cell. It may or may not be a precancerous indication associated with later malignancy, but the level of appropriate concern is highly dependent on the context with which it is diagnosed.
Lesion	A Lesion is any abnormal tissue found on or in an organism, usually damaged by disease or trauma. Lesion is derived from the Latin word laesio which means injury. Lesion s are caused by any process that damages tissues.
Leukemia	Leukemia is a cancer of the blood or bone marrow and is characterized by an abnormal proliferation (production by multiplication) of blood cells, usually white blood cells (leukocytes.) Leukemia is a broad term covering a spectrum of diseases. In turn, it is part of the even broader group of diseases called haematological neoplasms.
Giemsa stain	Giemsa stain an early malariologist, is used for the histopathological diagnosis of malaria and other parasites. It is specific for the phosphate groups of DNA and attaches itself to regions of DNA where there are high amounts of adenine-thymine bonding. Giemsa stain is used in Giemsa banding, commonly called G-banding, to stain chromosomes and often used to create an idiogram.
Trimethadione	Trimethadione is an oxazolidinedione anticonvulsant. It is used to treat epileptic conditions that are resistant to other treatments; recent studies by Doctor Jianxin Bao, Ph.D., at Washington University in Saint Louis"s Central Institute For The Deaf"s Center For Presbyacusis and Aging suggest that Trimethadione, along with other oxazolidinedione anticonvulsant medications may be useful in treating sensorineural hearing loss cases like those of Iraq war veterans- if the drug"s side effects, like dizziness, can be lessened by modifying the drug so it does not cross into the brain itself. If administered during pregnancy, fetal Trimethadione syndrome may result causing facial dysmorphism (short upturned nose, slanted eyebrows), cardiac defects, intrauterine growth retardation (IUGR), and mental retardation.
Platelet	Platelet s are small, irregularly-shaped anuclear cells (i.e. cells that do not have a nucleus containing DNA), 2-4 µm in diameter, which are derived from fragmentation of precursor megakaryocytes. The average lifespan of a Platelet is between 8 and 12 days. Platelet s play a fundamental role in hemostasis and are a natural source of growth factors.
Partial thromboplastin time	The Partial thromboplastin time or activated Partial thromboplastin time is a performance indicator measuring the efficacy of both the "intrinsic" (now referred to as the contact activation pathway) and the common coagulation pathways. Apart from detecting abnormalities in blood clotting, it is also used to monitor the treatment effects with heparin, a major anticoagulant. It is used in conjunction with the prothrombin time (PT) which measures the extrinsic pathway.
Retinitis pigmentosa	Retinitis pigmentosa is a group of genetic eye conditions. In the progression of symptoms for Retinitis pigmentosa, night blindness generally precedes tunnel vision by years or even decades. Many people with Retinitis pigmentosa do not become legally blind until their 40s or 50s and retain some sight all their lives .

Neoplasm	Neoplasm is an abnormal mass of tissue as a result of neoplasia. Neoplasia is the abnormal proliferation of cells. The growth of this clone of cells exceeds, and is uncoordinated with, that of the normal tissues around it.
Fibroepithelial neoplasms	Fibroepithelial neoplasms are biphasic tumors. This means they consist of epithelial tissue, and stromal or mesenchymal tissue. They may be benign or malignant.

Cancer	Cancer is a class of diseases in which a group of cells display uncontrolled growth (division beyond the normal limits), invasion (intrusion on and destruction of adjacent tissues), and sometimes metastasis (spread to other locations in the body via lymph or blood.) These three malignant properties of cancers differentiate them from benign tumors, which are self-limited, and do not invade or metastasize. Most cancers form a tumor but some, like leukemia, do not.
Stenosis	A Stenosis is an abnormal narrowing in a blood vessel or other tubular organ or structure. It is also sometimes called a "stricture" (as in urethral stricture.) The term "coarctation" is synonymous, but is commonly used only in the context of aortic coarctation.
Stroke	A Stroke is the rapidly developing loss of brain function(s) due to disturbance in the blood supply to the brain. This can be due to ischemia (lack of blood supply) caused by thrombosis or embolism or due to a hemorrhage. As a result, the affected area of the brain is unable to function, leading to inability to move one or more limbs on one side of the body, inability to understand or formulate speech, or inability to see one side of the visual field.
Schizophrenia	Schizophrenia , from the Greek roots skhizein and phrÄ"n, phren- (φρÎ®ν, φρεν-; "mind") is a psychiatric diagnosis that describes a mental disorder characterized by abnormalities in the perception or expression of reality. Distortions in perception may affect all five senses, including sight, hearing, taste, smell and touch, but most commonly manifest as auditory hallucinations, paranoid or bizarre delusions, or disorganized speech and thinking with significant social or occupational dysfunction. Onset of symptoms typically occurs in young adulthood, with approximately 0.4-0.6% of the population affected.
Infarction	In medicine, an Infarction is the process of tissue death (necrosis) caused by blockage of the tissue"s blood supply. The supplying artery may be blocked by an obstruction (e.g. an embolus, thrombus, or atherosclerotic plaque), may be mechanically compressed (e.g. tumor, volvulus, or hernia), ruptured by trauma (e.g. atherosclerosis or vasculitides), or vasoconstricted (e.g. cocaine vasoconstriction leading to myocardial Infarction) Infarction s are commonly associated with hypertension or atherosclerosis.

Chapter 6. Innate Immunity: Inflammation,

Inflammation	Inflammation is the complex biological response of vascular tissues to harmful stimuli, such as pathogens, damaged cells, or irritants. It is a protective attempt by the organism to remove the injurious stimuli as well as initiate the healing process for the tissue. Inflammation is not a synonym for infection.
Pathogenesis	The term Pathogenesis means step by step development of a disease and the chain of events leading to that disease due to a series of changes in the structure and /or function of a cell/tissue/organ being caused by a microbial, chemical or physical agent. The Pathogenesis of a disease is the mechanism by which an etiological factor causes the disease. The term can also be used to describe the development of the disease, such as acute, chronic and recurrent.
Platelet	Platelet s are small, irregularly-shaped anuclear cells (i.e. cells that do not have a nucleus containing DNA), 2-4 µm in diameter, which are derived from fragmentation of precursor megakaryocytes. The average lifespan of a Platelet is between 8 and 12 days. Platelet s play a fundamental role in hemostasis and are a natural source of growth factors.
Granuloma	Granuloma is a medical term for a ball-like collection of immune cells which forms when the immune system attempts to wall off substances that it perceives as foreign but is unable to eliminate. Such substances include infectious organisms such as bacteria and fungi as well as other materials such as keratin, suture fragments and vegetable particles. A Granuloma is therefore a special type of inflammatory reaction that can occur in a wide variety of diseases, both infectious and non-infectious.
Primary	In medicine, the reporting of symptoms by a patient may have significant psychological motivators. Psychologists sometimes categorize these motivators into primary or secondary gain. primary gain is internally good; motivationally.
Granulation tissue	Granulation tissue is the perfused, fibrous connective tissue that replaces a fibrin clot in healing wounds. Granulation tissue typically grows from the base of a wound and is able to fill wounds of almost any size it heals. Example of Granulation tissue from a cut on a finger with "proud flesh". During the proliferative phase of wound healing, Granulation tissue is: · light red or dark pink in color, being perfused (permeated) with new capillary loops or "buds"; · soft to the touch; · moist; and · bumpy (granular) in appearance. Granulation tissue is composed of tissue matrix supporting a variety of cell types, most of which can be associated with one of the following functions: · extracellular matrix, · immune system, or · vascularisation. An excess of Granulation tissue is informally referred to as "proud flesh." The extracellular matrix of Granulation tissue is created and modified by fibroblasts.

Hyperplasia

Hyperplasia is a general term referring to the proliferation of cells within an organ or tissue beyond that which is ordinarily seen (e.g. constantly dividing cells.) Hyperplasia may result in the gross enlargement of an organ, the formation of a benign tumor, or may be visible only under a microscope. Hyperplasia is different from hypertrophy in that the adaptive cell change in hypertrophy is by increased cellular size only, whereas in Hyperplasia it is by increased cellular number.

Cancer	Cancer is a class of diseases in which a group of cells display uncontrolled growth (division beyond the normal limits), invasion (intrusion on and destruction of adjacent tissues), and sometimes metastasis (spread to other locations in the body via lymph or blood.) These three malignant properties of cancers differentiate them from benign tumors, which are self-limited, and do not invade or metastasize. Most cancers form a tumor but some, like leukemia, do not.
Cluster of differentiation	The Cluster of differentiation is a protocol used for the identification and investigation of cell surface molecules present on leukocytes. CD molecules can act in numerous ways, often acting as receptors or ligands (the molecule that activates a receptor) important to the cell. A signal cascade is usually initiated, altering the behavior of the cell
Primary	In medicine, the reporting of symptoms by a patient may have significant psychological motivators. Psychologists sometimes categorize these motivators into primary or secondary gain. primary gain is internally good; motivationally.
Merozoite surface protein	A Merozoite surface protein is a protein molecule taken from the skin of a merozoite. A merozoite is a "daughter cell" of a protozoan. Merozoite surface protein s are useful in researching malaria, a disease caused by protozoans.
Pathophysiology	Pathophysiology is the study of the changes of normal mechanical, physical, and biochemical functions, either caused by a disease, or resulting from an abnormal syndrome. More formally, it is the branch of medicine which deals with any disturbances of body functions, caused by disease or prodromal symptoms. An alternate definition is "the study of the biological and physical manifestations of disease as they correlate with the underlying abnormalities and physiological disturbances." The study of pathology and the study of Pathophysiology often involves substantial overlap in diseases and processes, but pathology emphasizes direct observations, while Pathophysiology emphasizes quantifiable measurements.
Titer	A Titer is a measure of concentration. Titer testing employs serial dilution to obtain approximate quantitative information from an analytical procedure that inherently only evaluates as positive or negative. The Titer corresponds to the highest dilution factor that still yields a positive reading.
Neoplasm	Neoplasm is an abnormal mass of tissue as a result of neoplasia. Neoplasia is the abnormal proliferation of cells. The growth of this clone of cells exceeds, and is uncoordinated with, that of the normal tissues around it.

Blood test	A Blood test is a laboratory analysis performed on a blood sample that is usually extracted from a vein in the arm using a needle, or via fingerprick.
	Blood test s are used to determine physiological and biochemical states, such as disease, mineral content, drug effectiveness, and organ function. Although the term Blood test is used, most routine tests (except for most haematology) are done on plasma or serum, instead of blood cells.
Blindness	Blindness is the condition of lacking visual perception due to physiological or neurological factors. Various scales have been developed to describe the extent of vision loss and define Blindness. Total Blindness is the complete lack of form and visual light perception and is clinically recorded as NLP, an abbreviation for "no light perception." Blindness is frequently used to describe severe visual impairment with residual vision.
Amyloid	Amyloid s are insoluble fibrous protein aggregates sharing specific structural traits. Abnormal accumulation of Amyloid in organs may lead to Amyloid osis, and may play a role in various other neurodegenerative diseases.
	The name Amyloid comes from the early mistaken identification of the substance as starch , based on crude iodine-staining techniques.
Ferritin	Ferritin is a globular protein complex consisting of 24 protein subunits and is the primary intracellular iron-storage protein in both prokaryotes and eukaryotes, keeping iron in a soluble and non-toxic form. Ferritin that is not combined with iron is called apo Ferritin .
Hemolytic disease of the newborn	Hemolytic disease of the newborn HDN, HDFN is an alloimmune condition that develops in a fetus, when the IgG molecules that have been produced by the mother and have passed through the placenta include ones which attack the red blood cells in the fetal circulation. The red cells are broken down and the fetus can develop reticulocytosis and anaemia. This fetal disease ranges from mild to very severe, and fetal death from heart failure can occur.
Blood type	A Blood type is a classification of blood based on the presence or absence of inherited antigenic substances on the surface of red blood cells These antigens may be proteins, carbohydrates, glycoproteins depending on the blood group system, and some of these antigens are also present on the surface of other types of cells of various tissues. Several of these red blood cell surface antigens, that stem from one allele, collectively form a blood group system.
Transfusion reaction	In medicine, a Transfusion reaction is any adverse event which occurs because of a blood transfusion. These events can take the form of an allergic reaction, a transfusion-related infection, hemolysis related to an incompatible blood type, or an alteration of the immune system related to the transfusion. The risk of a Transfusion reaction must always be balanced against the anticipated benefit of a blood transfusion.

Cancer	Cancer is a class of diseases in which a group of cells display uncontrolled growth (division beyond the normal limits), invasion (intrusion on and destruction of adjacent tissues), and sometimes metastasis (spread to other locations in the body via lymph or blood.) These three malignant properties of cancers differentiate them from benign tumors, which are self-limited, and do not invade or metastasize. Most cancers form a tumor but some, like leukemia, do not.
Astrocytoma	Astrocytoma s are cancers of the brain that originate in star-shaped brain cells called astrocytes. They account for roughly 75% of neuroepithelial tumors. Of numerous grading systems in use, the most common is the World Health Organization (WHO) grading system for Astrocytoma
Idiopathic	Idiopathic is an adjective used primarily in medicine meaning arising spontaneously or from an obscure or unknown cause. From Greek á¼´διος, idios + πÎ¬θος, pathos (suffering), it means approximately "a disease of its own kind." It is technically a term from nosology, the classification of disease. For most medical conditions, one or more causes are somewhat understood, but in a certain percentage of people with the condition, the cause may not be readily apparent or characterized.
Pathogenesis	The term Pathogenesis means step by step development of a disease and the chain of events leading to that disease due to a series of changes in the structure and /or function of a cell/tissue/organ being caused by a microbial, chemical or physical agent. The Pathogenesis of a disease is the mechanism by which an etiological factor causes the disease. The term can also be used to describe the development of the disease, such as acute, chronic and recurrent.
Complete blood count	A Complete blood count is a test requested by a doctor or other medical professional that gives information about the cells in a patient"s blood. A scientist or lab technician performs the requested testing and provides the requesting Medical Professional with the results of the Complete blood count. Alexander Vastem is widely regarded as being the first person to use the Complete blood count for clinical purposes. Reference ranges used today stem from his clinical trials in the early 1960s.

Chapter 9. Infection,

Pathogenicity	Pathogenicity is the ability of a pathogen to produce an infectious disease in an organism. It is often used interchangeably with the term "virulence", although some authors prefer to reserve the latter term for descriptions of the relative degree of damage done by a pathogen. virulence is the ability of an organism to invade the bloodstream
Gram-positive	Gram-positive bacteria are those that are stained dark blue or violet by Gram staining. This is in contrast to Gram-negative bacteria, which cannot retain the crystal violet stain, instead taking up the counterstain (safranin or fuchsin) and appearing red or pink. Gram-positive organisms are able to retain the crystal violet stain because of the high amount of peptidoglycan in the cell wall.
Endotoxin	Endotoxin s (not to be confused with enterotoxin) are toxins associated with certain bacteria. Classically, an Endotoxin is a toxin that, unlike an "exotoxin", is not secreted in soluble form by live bacteria, but is a structural component in the bacteria which is released mainly when bacteria are lysed. Structure of a lipopolysaccharide The prototypical examples of Endotoxin are lipopolysaccharide (LPS) or lipo-oligo-saccharide (LOS) found in the outer membrane of various Gram-negative bacteria and is an important cause of their ability to cause disease.
Exotoxin	An Exotoxin is a toxin excreted by a microorganism, including bacteria, fungi, algae, and protozoa. An Exotoxin can cause damage to the host by destroying cells or disrupting normal cellular metabolism. They are highly potent and can cause major damage to the host.
Granuloma	Granuloma is a medical term for a ball-like collection of immune cells which forms when the immune system attempts to wall off substances that it perceives as foreign but is unable to eliminate. Such substances include infectious organisms such as bacteria and fungi as well as other materials such as keratin, suture fragments and vegetable particles. A Granuloma is therefore a special type of inflammatory reaction that can occur in a wide variety of diseases, both infectious and non-infectious.
Cancer	Cancer is a class of diseases in which a group of cells display uncontrolled growth (division beyond the normal limits), invasion (intrusion on and destruction of adjacent tissues), and sometimes metastasis (spread to other locations in the body via lymph or blood.) These three malignant properties of cancers differentiate them from benign tumors, which are self-limited, and do not invade or metastasize. Most cancers form a tumor but some, like leukemia, do not.
Mumps	Mumps or epidemic parotitis is a viral disease of the human species, caused by the Mumps virus. Prior to the development of vaccination and the introduction of a vaccine, it was a common childhood disease worldwide, and is still a significant threat to health in the third world. Painful swelling of the salivary glands (classically the parotid gland) is the most typical presentation.
Cholera	Cholera sometimes known as Asiatic or epidemic Cholera is an infectious gastroenteritis caused by enterotoxin-producing strains of the bacterium Vibrio Cholera e. Transmission to humans occurs through eating food or drinking water contaminated with Vibrio Cholera e from other Cholera patients. The major reservoir for Cholera was long assumed to be humans themselves, but considerable evidence exists that aquatic environments can serve as reservoirs of the bacteria.

Malaria

Malaria is a vector-borne infectious disease caused by protozoan parasites. It is widespread in tropical and subtropical regions, including parts of the Americas, Asia, and Africa. Each year, there are approximately 350-500 million cases of Malaria, killing between one and three million people, the majority of whom are young children in Sub-Saharan Africa.

Blindness	Blindness is the condition of lacking visual perception due to physiological or neurological factors. Various scales have been developed to describe the extent of vision loss and define Blindness. Total Blindness is the complete lack of form and visual light perception and is clinically recorded as NLP, an abbreviation for "no light perception." Blindness is frequently used to describe severe visual impairment with residual vision.
Seizure	An epileptic Seizure is a transient symptom of excessive or synchronous neuronal activity in the brain. It can manifest as an alteration in mental state, tonic or clonic movements, convulsions, and various other psychic symptoms (such as déjà vu or jamais vu.) The medical syndrome of recurrent, unprovoked Seizure s is termed epilepsy, but Seizure s can occur in people who do not have epilepsy.
Coombs test	Coombs test refers to two clinical blood tests used in immunohematology and immunology. The two Coombs tests are the direct Coombs test, and the indirect Coombs test
	In certain diseases or conditions an individual"s blood may contain IgG antibodies that can specifically bind to antigens on the red blood cell surface membrane, and their circulating red blood cells can become coated with IgG alloantibodies and/or IgG autoantibodies.

Cancer	Cancer is a class of diseases in which a group of cells display uncontrolled growth (division beyond the normal limits), invasion (intrusion on and destruction of adjacent tissues), and sometimes metastasis (spread to other locations in the body via lymph or blood.) These three malignant properties of cancers differentiate them from benign tumors, which are self-limited, and do not invade or metastasize. Most cancers form a tumor but some, like leukemia, do not.
Carcinoma	A Carcinoma is any malignant cancer that arises from epithelial cells. Carcinoma s invade surrounding tissues and organs and may metastasize, or spread, to lymph nodes and other sites.
Fibroepithelial neoplasms	Fibroepithelial neoplasms are biphasic tumors. This means they consist of epithelial tissue, and stromal or mesenchymal tissue. They may be benign or malignant.
Leiomyoma	A Leiomyoma (plural is " Leiomyoma ta") is a benign smooth muscle neoplasm that is not premalignant. They can occur in any organ, but the most common forms occur in the uterus, small bowel and the esophagus. · Greek: · leios = smooth · muV = mouse or muscle · oma = tumor · Latin: · Fibra = fiber Leiomyoma enucleated from a uterus. External surface on left; cut surface on right Uterine fibroids are Leiomyoma ta of the uterine smooth muscle.
Dysplasia	Dysplasia is a term used in pathology to refer to an abnormality in maturation of cells within a tissue. This generally consists of an expansion of immature cells, with a corresponding decrease in the number and location of mature cells. Dysplasia is often indicative of an early neoplastic process.
Sarcoma	A Sarcoma is a cancer of the connective tissue resulting in mesoderm proliferation. This is in contrast to carcinomas, which are of epithelial origin (breast, colon, pancreas, and others.) However, due to an evolving understanding of tissue origin, the term "Sarcoma" is sometimes applied to tumors now known to arise from epithelial tissue.
High-grade prostatic intraepithelial neoplasia	In urologic pathology, High-grade prostatic intraepithelial neoplasia, abbreviated HGPIN, is an abnormality of prostatic glands and believed to precede the development of prostate adenocarcinoma (the most common form of prostate cancer.) It is considered to be a pre-malignancy of the prostatic glands. On a subsequent biopsy, given a history of a HGPIN diagnosis, the chance of finding prostatic adenocarcinoma is approximately 30%.

Leukemia	Leukemia is a cancer of the blood or bone marrow and is characterized by an abnormal proliferation (production by multiplication) of blood cells, usually white blood cells (leukocytes.) Leukemia is a broad term covering a spectrum of diseases. In turn, it is part of the even broader group of diseases called haematological neoplasms.
Tumor marker	A Tumor marker is a substance found in the blood, urine among other tissue types. There are many different Tumor marker s, each indicative of a particular disease process, and they are used in oncology to help detect the presence of cancer. An elevated level of a Tumor marker can indicate cancer; however, there can also be other causes of the elevation.
Blood test	A Blood test is a laboratory analysis performed on a blood sample that is usually extracted from a vein in the arm using a needle, or via fingerprick. Blood test s are used to determine physiological and biochemical states, such as disease, mineral content, drug effectiveness, and organ function. Although the term Blood test is used, most routine tests (except for most haematology) are done on plasma or serum, instead of blood cells.
Rapid plasma reagin	Rapid plasma reagin refers to a type of test that looks for non-specific antibodies in the blood of the patient that may indicate that the organism (Treponema pallidum) that causes syphilis is present. The term "reagin" means that this test does not look for antibodies against the actual bacterium, but rather for antibodies against substances released by cells when they are damaged by T. pallidum. Another test often used to screen for syphilis is the Venereal Disease Research Laboratory VDRL slide test.
Inflammation	Inflammation is the complex biological response of vascular tissues to harmful stimuli, such as pathogens, damaged cells, or irritants. It is a protective attempt by the organism to remove the injurious stimuli as well as initiate the healing process for the tissue. Inflammation is not a synonym for infection.
Lesion	A Lesion is any abnormal tissue found on or in an organism, usually damaged by disease or trauma. Lesion is derived from the Latin word laesio which means injury. Lesion s are caused by any process that damages tissues.
Ann Arbor staging	Ann Arbor staging is the staging system for lymphomas, both in Hodgkin"s lymphoma (previously called Hodgkin"s Disease) and Non-Hodgkin lymphoma It was initially developed for Hodgkin"s, but has some use in NHL. It has roughly the same function as TNM staging in solid tumors. The stage depends on both the place where the malignant tissue is located (as located with biopsy, CT scanning and increasingly positron emission tomography) and on systemic symptoms due to the lymphoma ("B symptoms": night sweats, weight loss of >10% or fevers.)
Screening	The risk of transmitting HIV infection to blood transfusion recipients has been drastically reduced by improved donor selection and sensitive serologic screening assays in many countries. In 2000, WHO estimated that 1 million new HIV infections around the world resulted from inadequate blood screening.

screening tests require a high degree of confidence that HIV is not present, so a combination of antibody (serology), antigen and nucleic acid based tests are used by blood banks in Western countries.

Carcinoembryonic antigen	Carcinoembryonic antigen is a glycoprotein involved in cell adhesion. It is normally produced during fetal development, but the production of CEA stops before birth. Therefore, it is not usually present in the blood of healthy adults, although levels are raised in heavy smokers.
Basal cell carcinoma	Basal cell carcinoma is the most common type of skin cancer. It rarely metastasizes or kills, but it is still considered malignant because it can cause significant destruction and disfigurement by invading surrounding tissues. Statistically, approximately 3 out of 10 Caucasians develop a basal cell cancer within their lifetime.
Squamous cell carcinoma	In medicine, Squamous cell carcinoma is a form of cancer of the carcinoma type that may occur in many different organs, including the skin, lips, mouth, esophagus, urinary bladder, prostate, lungs, vagina, and cervix. It is a malignant tumor of squamous epithelium (epithelium that shows squamous cell differentiation.) Squamous cell carcinoma may be classified into the following types:[473] · Adenoid Squamous cell carcinoma · Clear cell Squamous cell carcinoma (Clear cell carcinoma of the skin) · Spindle cell Squamous cell carcinoma · Signet-ring cell Squamous cell carcinoma · Basaloid Squamous cell carcinoma · Verrucous carcinoma · Keratoacanthoma A large Squamous cell carcinoma of the tongue. A carcinoma can be characterized as either in situ (confined to the original site) or invasive, depending on whether the cancer invades underlying tissues; only invasive cancers are able to spread to other organs and cause metastasis. Squamous cell carcinoma in situ are also called Bowen"s disease.
Benzene	Benzene, or benzol, is an organic chemical compound and a known carcinogen with the molecular formula C_6H_6. It is sometimes abbreviated Ph-H. Benzene is a colorless and highly flammable liquid with a sweet smell and a relatively high melting point. Because it is a known carcinogen, its use as an additive in gasoline is now limited, but it is an important industrial solvent and precursor in the production of drugs, plastics, synthetic rubber, and dyes.
Diagnosis	In medicine, diagnosis is the process of identifying a medical condition or disease by its signs, symptoms, and from the results of various diagnostic procedures. The conclusion reached through this process is called a diagnosis. The term "diagnostic criteria" designates the combination of signs, symptoms, and test results that allows the doctor to ascertain the diagnosis of the respective disease.

Cancer	Cancer is a class of diseases in which a group of cells display uncontrolled growth (division beyond the normal limits), invasion (intrusion on and destruction of adjacent tissues), and sometimes metastasis (spread to other locations in the body via lymph or blood.) These three malignant properties of cancers differentiate them from benign tumors, which are self-limited, and do not invade or metastasize. Most cancers form a tumor but some, like leukemia, do not.
Carcinoma	A Carcinoma is any malignant cancer that arises from epithelial cells. Carcinoma s invade surrounding tissues and organs and may metastasize, or spread, to lymph nodes and other sites.
Fibroepithelial neoplasms	Fibroepithelial neoplasms are biphasic tumors. This means they consist of epithelial tissue, and stromal or mesenchymal tissue. They may be benign or malignant.
Ann Arbor staging	Ann Arbor staging is the staging system for lymphomas, both in Hodgkin"s lymphoma (previously called Hodgkin"s Disease) and Non-Hodgkin lymphoma It was initially developed for Hodgkin"s, but has some use in NHL. It has roughly the same function as TNM staging in solid tumors. The stage depends on both the place where the malignant tissue is located (as located with biopsy, CT scanning and increasingly positron emission tomography) and on systemic symptoms due to the lymphoma ("B symptoms": night sweats, weight loss of >10% or fevers.)
Inflammation	Inflammation is the complex biological response of vascular tissues to harmful stimuli, such as pathogens, damaged cells, or irritants. It is a protective attempt by the organism to remove the injurious stimuli as well as initiate the healing process for the tissue. Inflammation is not a synonym for infection.
Pathogenesis	The term Pathogenesis means step by step development of a disease and the chain of events leading to that disease due to a series of changes in the structure and /or function of a cell/tissue/organ being caused by a microbial, chemical or physical agent. The Pathogenesis of a disease is the mechanism by which an etiological factor causes the disease. The term can also be used to describe the development of the disease, such as acute, chronic and recurrent.
Primary	In medicine, the reporting of symptoms by a patient may have significant psychological motivators. Psychologists sometimes categorize these motivators into primary or secondary gain. primary gain is internally good; motivationally.
Lymphatic system	The Lymphatic system in vertebrates is a network of conduits that carry a clear fluid called lymph. It also includes the lymphoid tissue through which the lymph travels. Lymphoid tissue is found in many organs, particularly the lymph nodes, and in the lymphoid follicles associated with the digestive system such as the tonsils.

Cachexia	Cachexia is loss of weight, muscle atrophy, fatigue, weakness and significant loss of appetite in someone who is not actively trying to lose weight. The formal definition of Cachexia is the loss of body mass that cannot be reversed nutritionally; even if you supplement the patient calorically, lean body mass will be lost, indicating there is a fundamental pathology in place. Cachexia is seen in patients with cancer, AIDS, COPD (chronic obstructive pulmonary disease), and CHF (congestive heart failure.)
Leukemia	Leukemia is a cancer of the blood or bone marrow and is characterized by an abnormal proliferation (production by multiplication) of blood cells, usually white blood cells (leukocytes.) Leukemia is a broad term covering a spectrum of diseases. In turn, it is part of the even broader group of diseases called haematological neoplasms.

Cancer	Cancer is a class of diseases in which a group of cells display uncontrolled growth (division beyond the normal limits), invasion (intrusion on and destruction of adjacent tissues), and sometimes metastasis (spread to other locations in the body via lymph or blood.) These three malignant properties of cancers differentiate them from benign tumors, which are self-limited, and do not invade or metastasize. Most cancers form a tumor but some, like leukemia, do not.
Carcinoma	A Carcinoma is any malignant cancer that arises from epithelial cells. Carcinoma s invade surrounding tissues and organs and may metastasize, or spread, to lymph nodes and other sites.
Fibroepithelial neoplasms	Fibroepithelial neoplasms are biphasic tumors. This means they consist of epithelial tissue, and stromal or mesenchymal tissue. They may be benign or malignant.
Etiology	Etiology is the study of causation, or origination. The word is most commonly used in medical and philosophical theories, where it is used to refer to the study of why things occur, or even the reasons behind the way that things act, and is used in philosophy, physics, psychology, government, medicine, theology and biology in reference to the causes of various phenomena. An etiological myth is a myth intended to explain a name or create a mythic history for a place or family.

Primary	In medicine, the reporting of symptoms by a patient may have significant psychological motivators. Psychologists sometimes categorize these motivators into primary or secondary gain.
	primary gain is internally good; motivationally.
Dieldrin	Dieldrin is a chlorinated hydrocarbon originally produced in 1948 by J. Hyman ' Co, Denver, as an insecticide. The molecule has a ring structure based on naphthalene.
	Dieldrin is closely related to aldrin which itself breaks down to form Dieldrin.
Stroke	A Stroke is the rapidly developing loss of brain function(s) due to disturbance in the blood supply to the brain. This can be due to ischemia (lack of blood supply) caused by thrombosis or embolism or due to a hemorrhage. As a result, the affected area of the brain is unable to function, leading to inability to move one or more limbs on one side of the body, inability to understand or formulate speech, or inability to see one side of the visual field.
Hematoma	A Hematoma is a collection of blood outside the blood vessels, generally the result of hemorrhage internal bleeding.
	It is not to be confused with hemangioma which is an abnormal build up of blood vessels in the skin or internal organs.
	Hematoma - from Greek αἷμα, haima, blood + τωμα, t-oma, indicating an abnormality.
Stenosis	A Stenosis is an abnormal narrowing in a blood vessel or other tubular organ or structure.
	It is also sometimes called a "stricture" (as in urethral stricture.)
	The term "coarctation" is synonymous, but is commonly used only in the context of aortic coarctation.
Acetazolamide	Acetazolamide, sold under the trade name Diamox, is a carbonic anhydrase inhibitor that is used to treat glaucoma, epileptic seizures, benign intracranial hypertension (pseudotumor cerebri), altitude sickness, cystinuria, and dural ectasia. Acetazolamide is available as a generic drug and is also used as a diuretic.
	This drug is a carbonic anhydrase inhibitor.
Senile plaques	Senile plaques are extracellular deposits of amyloid in the gray matter of the brain. The deposits are associated with degenerative neural structures and an abundance of microglia and astrocytes.
Gingivitis	Gingivitis around the teeth is a general term for gingival diseases affecting the gingiva As generally used, the term Gingivitis refers to gingival inflammation induced by bacterial biofilms adherent to tooth surfaces.
	Gingivitis can be defined as inflammation of the gingival tissue without loss of tooth attachment
Neurofibrillary tangles	Neurofibrillary tangles are pathological protein aggregates found within neurons in cases of Alzheimer"s disease. They were first described by Alois Alzheimer in one of his patients suffering from the disorder (at the time it was not called Alzheimer"s disease.) Tangles are formed by hyperphosphorylation of a microtubule-associated protein known as tau, causing it to aggregate in an insoluble form.

Aneurysm	An Aneurysm (or aneurism) is a localized, blood-filled dilation of a blood vessel caused by disease or weakening of the vessel wall.
	Aneurysm s most commonly occur in arteries at the base of the brain (the circle of Willis) and in the aorta (the main artery coming out of the heart, a so-called aortic Aneurysm) As the size of an Aneurysm increases, there is an increased risk of rupture, which can result in severe hemorrhage or other complications including sudden death.
Cancer	Cancer is a class of diseases in which a group of cells display uncontrolled growth (division beyond the normal limits), invasion (intrusion on and destruction of adjacent tissues), and sometimes metastasis (spread to other locations in the body via lymph or blood.) These three malignant properties of cancers differentiate them from benign tumors, which are self-limited, and do not invade or metastasize. Most cancers form a tumor but some, like leukemia, do not.
Fibroepithelial neoplasms	Fibroepithelial neoplasms are biphasic tumors. This means they consist of epithelial tissue, and stromal or mesenchymal tissue. They may be benign or malignant.
Pathogenesis	The term Pathogenesis means step by step development of a disease and the chain of events leading to that disease due to a series of changes in the structure and /or function of a cell/tissue/organ being caused by a microbial, chemical or physical agent. The Pathogenesis of a disease is the mechanism by which an etiological factor causes the disease. The term can also be used to describe the development of the disease, such as acute, chronic and recurrent.
Stroke	A Stroke is the rapidly developing loss of brain function(s) due to disturbance in the blood supply to the brain. This can be due to ischemia (lack of blood supply) caused by thrombosis or embolism or due to a hemorrhage. As a result, the affected area of the brain is unable to function, leading to inability to move one or more limbs on one side of the body, inability to understand or formulate speech, or inability to see one side of the visual field.
Intracranial hemorrhage	An Intracranial hemorrhage is a hemorrhage within the skull.
	Intracranial bleeding occurs when a blood vessel within the skull is ruptured or leaks. It can result from physical trauma (as occurs in head injury) or nontraumatic causes (as occurs in hemorrhagic stroke) such as a ruptured aneurysm.
Bleeding time	Bleeding time is a medical test done on someone to assess their platelet function.
	The term "template Bleeding time" is used when the test is performed to standardized parameters. This makes it easier to compare data collected at different facilities.
Pathophysiology	Pathophysiology is the study of the changes of normal mechanical, physical, and biochemical functions, either caused by a disease, or resulting from an abnormal syndrome. More formally, it is the branch of medicine which deals with any disturbances of body functions, caused by disease or prodromal symptoms.
	An alternate definition is "the study of the biological and physical manifestations of disease as they correlate with the underlying abnormalities and physiological disturbances."

The study of pathology and the study of Pathophysiology often involves substantial overlap in diseases and processes, but pathology emphasizes direct observations, while Pathophysiology emphasizes quantifiable measurements.

Trachoma

Trachoma is an infectious eye disease, and the leading cause of the world"s infectious blindness. Globally, 84 million people suffer from active infection and nearly 8 million people are visually impaired as a result of this disease. Globally this disease results in considerable disability.

Stenosis

A Stenosis is an abnormal narrowing in a blood vessel or other tubular organ or structure.
It is also sometimes called a "stricture" (as in urethral stricture.)
The term "coarctation" is synonymous, but is commonly used only in the context of aortic coarctation.

Cataract

A Cataract is a clouding that develops in the crystalline lens of the eye or in its envelope, varying in degree from slight to complete opacity and obstructing the passage of light. Early in the development of age-related Cataract the power of the lens may be increased, causing near-sightedness (myopia), and the gradual yellowing and opacification of the lens may reduce the perception of blue colours. Cataract s typically progress slowly to cause vision loss and are potentially blinding if untreated.

Glaucoma

Glaucoma refers to a group of diseases that affect the optic nerve and involves a loss of retinal ganglion cells in a characteristic pattern. It is a type of optic neuropathy. Raised intraocular pressure is a significant risk factor for developing Glaucoma

Blindness

Blindness is the condition of lacking visual perception due to physiological or neurological factors. Various scales have been developed to describe the extent of vision loss and define Blindness. Total Blindness is the complete lack of form and visual light perception and is clinically recorded as NLP, an abbreviation for "no light perception." Blindness is frequently used to describe severe visual impairment with residual vision.

Aura

An Aura is the perceptual disturbance experienced by some migraine sufferers before a migraine headache, and the telltale sensation experienced by some people with epilepsy before a seizure. It often manifests as the perception of a strange light, an unpleasant smell or confusing thoughts or experiences.
When occurring, auras allow epileptics time to prevent injury to themselves.

Pathophysiology	Pathophysiology is the study of the changes of normal mechanical, physical, and biochemical functions, either caused by a disease, or resulting from an abnormal syndrome. More formally, it is the branch of medicine which deals with any disturbances of body functions, caused by disease or prodromal symptoms. An alternate definition is "the study of the biological and physical manifestations of disease as they correlate with the underlying abnormalities and physiological disturbances." The study of pathology and the study of Pathophysiology often involves substantial overlap in diseases and processes, but pathology emphasizes direct observations, while Pathophysiology emphasizes quantifiable measurements.
Brain death	Brain death is a legal definition of death that refers to the irreversible end of all brain activity (including involuntary activity necessary to sustain life) due to total necrosis of the cerebral neurons following loss of blood flow and oxygenation. It should not be confused with a persistent vegetative state. The concept of Brain death emerged in the 1960s, as the ability to resuscitate individuals and mechanically keep the heart and lungs functioning became prevalent.
Cancer	Cancer is a class of diseases in which a group of cells display uncontrolled growth (division beyond the normal limits), invasion (intrusion on and destruction of adjacent tissues), and sometimes metastasis (spread to other locations in the body via lymph or blood.) These three malignant properties of cancers differentiate them from benign tumors, which are self-limited, and do not invade or metastasize. Most cancers form a tumor but some, like leukemia, do not.
Primary	In medicine, the reporting of symptoms by a patient may have significant psychological motivators. Psychologists sometimes categorize these motivators into primary or secondary gain. primary gain is internally good; motivationally.
Seizure	An epileptic Seizure is a transient symptom of excessive or synchronous neuronal activity in the brain. It can manifest as an alteration in mental state, tonic or clonic movements, convulsions, and various other psychic symptoms (such as déjà vu or jamais vu.) The medical syndrome of recurrent, unprovoked Seizure s is termed epilepsy, but Seizure s can occur in people who do not have epilepsy.
Postictal state	The Postictal state is the altered state of consciousness that a person enters after experiencing an epileptic seizure, such as those occurring with frontal lobe epilepsy. It usually lasts between 5 and 30 minutes, but sometimes longer in the case of larger or more severe seizures and is characterized by drowsiness, confusion, nausea, hypertension, headache or migraine and other disorienting symptoms. Additionally, emergence from this period is often accompanied by amnesia or other memory defects.
Status epilepticus	Status epilepticus refers to a life-threatening condition in which the brain is in a state of persistent seizure. Definitions vary, but traditionally it is defined as one continuous unremitting seizure lasting longer than 30 minutes , or recurrent seizures without regaining consciousness between seizures for greater than 30 minutes. There is some evidence that 5 minutes is sufficient to damage neurons and that seizures are unlikely to self-terminate by that time.

55

Aura	An Aura is the perceptual disturbance experienced by some migraine sufferers before a migraine headache, and the telltale sensation experienced by some people with epilepsy before a seizure. It often manifests as the perception of a strange light, an unpleasant smell or confusing thoughts or experiences.
	When occurring, auras allow epileptics time to prevent injury to themselves.
Idiopathic	Idiopathic is an adjective used primarily in medicine meaning arising spontaneously or from an obscure or unknown cause. From Greek á¼´διος, idios + πΊ¬θος, pathos (suffering), it means approximately "a disease of its own kind."
	It is technically a term from nosology, the classification of disease. For most medical conditions, one or more causes are somewhat understood, but in a certain percentage of people with the condition, the cause may not be readily apparent or characterized.
Atrophy	Atrophy is the partial or complete wasting away of a part of the body. Causes of Atrophy include poor nourishment, poor circulation, loss of hormonal support, loss of nerve supply to the target organ, disuse or lack of exercise or disease intrinsic to the tissue itself. Hormonal and nerve inputs that maintain an organ or body part are referred to as trophic.
Stenosis	A Stenosis is an abnormal narrowing in a blood vessel or other tubular organ or structure.
	It is also sometimes called a "stricture" (as in urethral stricture.)
	The term "coarctation" is synonymous, but is commonly used only in the context of aortic coarctation.
Lewy bodies	Lewy bodies are abnormal aggregates of protein that develop inside nerve cells. They are identified under the microscope when histology is performed on the brain.
	Lewy bodies appear as spherical masses that displace other cell components.
Senile plaques	Senile plaques are extracellular deposits of amyloid in the gray matter of the brain. The deposits are associated with degenerative neural structures and an abundance of microglia and astrocytes.
Gingivitis	Gingivitis around the teeth is a general term for gingival diseases affecting the gingiva As generally used, the term Gingivitis refers to gingival inflammation induced by bacterial biofilms adherent to tooth surfaces.
	Gingivitis can be defined as inflammation of the gingival tissue without loss of tooth attachment
Neurofibrillary tangles	Neurofibrillary tangles are pathological protein aggregates found within neurons in cases of Alzheimer"s disease. They were first described by Alois Alzheimer in one of his patients suffering from the disorder (at the time it was not called Alzheimer"s disease.) Tangles are formed by hyperphosphorylation of a microtubule-associated protein known as tau, causing it to aggregate in an insoluble form.

Hydrocephalus	Hydrocephalus is a term derived from the Greek words "hydro" meaning water, and "cephalus" meaning head, and this condition is sometimes known as "water on the brain". People with Hydrocephalus have abnormal accumulation of cerebrospinal fluid in the ventricles, or cavities, of the brain. This may cause increased intracranial pressure inside the skull and progressive enlargement of the head, convulsion, and mental disability.
Fibroepithelial neoplasms	Fibroepithelial neoplasms are biphasic tumors. This means they consist of epithelial tissue, and stromal or mesenchymal tissue. They may be benign or malignant.
Diagnosis	In medicine, diagnosis is the process of identifying a medical condition or disease by its signs, symptoms, and from the results of various diagnostic procedures. The conclusion reached through this process is called a diagnosis. The term "diagnostic criteria" designates the combination of signs, symptoms, and test results that allows the doctor to ascertain the diagnosis of the respective disease.
Astrocytoma	Astrocytoma s are cancers of the brain that originate in star-shaped brain cells called astrocytes. They account for roughly 75% of neuroepithelial tumors. Of numerous grading systems in use, the most common is the World Health Organization (WHO) grading system for Astrocytoma

Cancer	Cancer is a class of diseases in which a group of cells display uncontrolled growth (division beyond the normal limits), invasion (intrusion on and destruction of adjacent tissues), and sometimes metastasis (spread to other locations in the body via lymph or blood.) These three malignant properties of cancers differentiate them from benign tumors, which are self-limited, and do not invade or metastasize. Most cancers form a tumor but some, like leukemia, do not.
Hematoma	A Hematoma is a collection of blood outside the blood vessels, generally the result of hemorrhage internal bleeding.
	It is not to be confused with hemangioma which is an abnormal build up of blood vessels in the skin or internal organs.
	Hematoma - from Greek αἶμα, haima, blood + τωμα, t-oma, indicating an abnormality.
Pathophysiology	Pathophysiology is the study of the changes of normal mechanical, physical, and biochemical functions, either caused by a disease, or resulting from an abnormal syndrome. More formally, it is the branch of medicine which deals with any disturbances of body functions, caused by disease or prodromal symptoms.
	An alternate definition is "the study of the biological and physical manifestations of disease as they correlate with the underlying abnormalities and physiological disturbances."
	The study of pathology and the study of Pathophysiology often involves substantial overlap in diseases and processes, but pathology emphasizes direct observations, while Pathophysiology emphasizes quantifiable measurements.
Primary	In medicine, the reporting of symptoms by a patient may have significant psychological motivators. Psychologists sometimes categorize these motivators into primary or secondary gain.
	primary gain is internally good; motivationally.
Stenosis	A Stenosis is an abnormal narrowing in a blood vessel or other tubular organ or structure.
	It is also sometimes called a "stricture" (as in urethral stricture.)
	The term "coarctation" is synonymous, but is commonly used only in the context of aortic coarctation.
Glaucoma	Glaucoma refers to a group of diseases that affect the optic nerve and involves a loss of retinal ganglion cells in a characteristic pattern. It is a type of optic neuropathy. Raised intraocular pressure is a significant risk factor for developing Glaucoma
Infarction	In medicine, an Infarction is the process of tissue death (necrosis) caused by blockage of the tissue"s blood supply. The supplying artery may be blocked by an obstruction (e.g. an embolus, thrombus, or atherosclerotic plaque), may be mechanically compressed (e.g. tumor, volvulus, or hernia), ruptured by trauma (e.g. atherosclerosis or vasculitides), or vasoconstricted (e.g. cocaine vasoconstriction leading to myocardial Infarction)
	Infarction s are commonly associated with hypertension or atherosclerosis.

Pathogenesis	The term Pathogenesis means step by step development of a disease and the chain of events leading to that disease due to a series of changes in the structure and /or function of a cell/tissue/organ being caused by a microbial, chemical or physical agent. The Pathogenesis of a disease is the mechanism by which an etiological factor causes the disease. The term can also be used to describe the development of the disease, such as acute, chronic and recurrent.
Stroke	A Stroke is the rapidly developing loss of brain function(s) due to disturbance in the blood supply to the brain. This can be due to ischemia (lack of blood supply) caused by thrombosis or embolism or due to a hemorrhage. As a result, the affected area of the brain is unable to function, leading to inability to move one or more limbs on one side of the body, inability to understand or formulate speech, or inability to see one side of the visual field.
Cerebral hemorrhage	A Cerebral hemorrhage (or intra Cerebral hemorrhage , I Cerebral hemorrhage), is a subtype of intracranial hemorrhage that occurs within the brain tissue itself. Intra Cerebral hemorrhage can be caused by brain trauma, or it can occur spontaneously in hemorrhagic stroke. Non-traumatic intracerebral haemorrhage is a spontaneous bleeding into the brain tissue.
Cerebral infarction	A Cerebral infarction is the ischemic kind of stroke due to a disturbance in the blood vessels supplying blood to the brain. It can be atherothrombotic or embolic. From stroke caused by Cerebral infarction two other kinds of stroke should be distinguished: cerebral hemorrhage and subarachnoid hemorrhage.
Lacunar stroke	Lacunar stroke or lacunar infarct (LACI) is a type of stroke that results from occlusion of one of the penetrating arteries that provides blood to the brain"s deep structures. Patients who present with symptoms of a Lacunar stroke but who have not yet had diagnostic imaging performed may be described as suffering from Lacunar stroke Syndrome (LACS.) Much of the current knowledge of Lacunar stroke s comes from C. M. Fisher"s cadaver dissections of post-mortem stroke patients.
Aneurysm	An Aneurysm (or aneurism) is a localized, blood-filled dilation of a blood vessel caused by disease or weakening of the vessel wall. Aneurysm s most commonly occur in arteries at the base of the brain (the circle of Willis) and in the aorta (the main artery coming out of the heart, a so-called aortic Aneurysm) As the size of an Aneurysm increases, there is an increased risk of rupture, which can result in severe hemorrhage or other complications including sudden death.
Toxoplasmosis	Toxoplasmosis is a parasitic disease caused by the protozoan Toxoplasma gondii. The parasite infects most genera of warm-blooded animals, including humans, but the primary host is the felid (cat) family. Animals are infected by eating infected meat, by ingestion of feces of a cat that has itself recently been infected, or by transmission from mother to fetus.
Arteriovenous malformation	Arteriovenous malformation or AVM is an abnormal connection between veins and arteries, usually congenital. This pathology is widely known because of its occurrence in the central nervous system, but can appear in any location.

The genetic transmission patterns of AVM, if any, are unknown.

Acoustic neuroma	An Acoustic neuroma is a benign primary intracranial tumor of the myelin-forming cells of the vestibulocochlear nerve The term "acoustic" is a misnomer, as the tumor rarely arises from the acoustic division of the vestibulocochlear nerve. The correct medical term is vestibular schwannoma, because it involves the vestibular portion of the 8th cranial nerve and it arises from Schwann cells, which are responsible for the myelin sheath in the peripheral nervous system.
Fibroepithelial neoplasms	Fibroepithelial neoplasms are biphasic tumors. This means they consist of epithelial tissue, and stromal or mesenchymal tissue. They may be benign or malignant.
Astrocytoma	Astrocytoma s are cancers of the brain that originate in star-shaped brain cells called astrocytes. They account for roughly 75% of neuroepithelial tumors. Of numerous grading systems in use, the most common is the World Health Organization (WHO) grading system for Astrocytoma
Carcinoma	A Carcinoma is any malignant cancer that arises from epithelial cells. Carcinoma s invade surrounding tissues and organs and may metastasize, or spread, to lymph nodes and other sites.
Liquefactive necrosis	Liquefactive necrosis is a type of necrosis which is characteristic of focal bacterial or fungal infections. In Liquefactive necrosis, the affected cell is completely digested by hydrolytic enzymes, resulting in a soft, circumscribed lesion consisting of pus and the fluid remains of necrotic tissue. After the removal of cell debris by white blood cells, a fluid filled space is left.
Inflammation	Inflammation is the complex biological response of vascular tissues to harmful stimuli, such as pathogens, damaged cells, or irritants. It is a protective attempt by the organism to remove the injurious stimuli as well as initiate the healing process for the tissue. Inflammation is not a synonym for infection.
Brain abscess	Brain abscess is an abscess caused by inflammation and collection of infected material, coming from local (ear infection, dental abscess, infection of paranasal sinuses, infection of the mastoid air cells of the temporal bone, epidural abscess) or remote (lung, heart, kidney etc.) infectious sources, within the brain tissue. The infection may also be introduced through a skull fracture following a head trauma or surgical procedures.
Idiopathic	Idiopathic is an adjective used primarily in medicine meaning arising spontaneously or from an obscure or unknown cause. From Greek á¼´διος, idios + πῖ¬θος, pathos (suffering), it means approximately "a disease of its own kind." It is technically a term from nosology, the classification of disease. For most medical conditions, one or more causes are somewhat understood, but in a certain percentage of people with the condition, the cause may not be readily apparent or characterized.

| Cholinergic crisis | A Cholinergic crisis is an over-stimulation at a neuromuscular junction due to an excess of acetylcholine (ACh), as of a result of the inactivity (perhaps even inhibition) of the AChE enzyme, which normally breaks down acetylcholine. This is a consequence of some types of nerve gas. In medicine, this is seen in patients with myasthenia gravis who take too high a dose of their cholinergic treatment medications, or seen in some surgical cases, when too high a dose of a cholinesterase inhibitor is given to reverse surgical muscle paralysis. |

Schizophrenia	Schizophrenia , from the Greek roots skhizein and phrÄ"n, phren- (φρÎ®ν, φρεν-; "mind") is a psychiatric diagnosis that describes a mental disorder characterized by abnormalities in the perception or expression of reality. Distortions in perception may affect all five senses, including sight, hearing, taste, smell and touch, but most commonly manifest as auditory hallucinations, paranoid or bizarre delusions, or disorganized speech and thinking with significant social or occupational dysfunction. Onset of symptoms typically occurs in young adulthood, with approximately 0.4-0.6% of the population affected.
Etiology	Etiology is the study of causation, or origination. The word is most commonly used in medical and philosophical theories, where it is used to refer to the study of why things occur, or even the reasons behind the way that things act, and is used in philosophy, physics, psychology, government, medicine, theology and biology in reference to the causes of various phenomena. An etiological myth is a myth intended to explain a name or create a mythic history for a place or family.
Pathophysiology	Pathophysiology is the study of the changes of normal mechanical, physical, and biochemical functions, either caused by a disease, or resulting from an abnormal syndrome. More formally, it is the branch of medicine which deals with any disturbances of body functions, caused by disease or prodromal symptoms. An alternate definition is "the study of the biological and physical manifestations of disease as they correlate with the underlying abnormalities and physiological disturbances." The study of pathology and the study of Pathophysiology often involves substantial overlap in diseases and processes, but pathology emphasizes direct observations, while Pathophysiology emphasizes quantifiable measurements.
Delusion	A Delusion, in everyday language, is a fixed belief that is either false, fanciful, or derived from deception. Psychiatry defines the term more specifically as a belief that is pathological (the result of an illness or illness process.) As a pathology, it is distinct from a belief based on false or incomplete information, apperception, illusion, or other effects of perception.
Bipolar disorder	Bipolar disorder manic depressive disorder or bipolar affective disorder, is a psychiatric diagnosis that describes a category of mood disorders defined by the presence of one or more episodes of abnormally elevated mood clinically referred to as mania or, if milder, hypomania. Individuals who experience manic episodes also commonly experience depressive episodes or symptoms, or mixed episodes in which features of both mania and depression are present at the same time. These episodes are usually separated by periods of "normal" mood, but in some individuals, depression and mania may rapidly alternate, known as rapid cycling.
Reuptake inhibitor	A Reuptake inhibitor is a drug which inhibits the plasmalemmal transporter-mediated reuptake of a neurotransmitter from the synapse into the pre-synaptic neuron, leading to an increase in the extracellular concentrations of the neurotransmitter and therefore an increase in neurotransmission. Many drugs utilize reuptake inhibition to exert their psychological and physiological effects, including various antidepressants, anxiolytics, stimulants, and anorectics, among others. Most known Reuptake inhibitor s affect the monoamine neurotransmitters serotonin, norepinephrine, and dopamine.

Lamotrigine	Lamotrigine by GlaxoSmithKline, called Lamictin in South Africa, ×œ×ž×•×'"×™×Ÿ in Israel, and ë¼ë¯'ìf˜ in South Korea and also Lamitor) is an anticonvulsant drug used in the treatment of epilepsy and bipolar disorder. For epilepsy it is used to treat partial seizures, primary and secondary tonic-clonic seizures, and seizures associated with Lennox-Gastaut syndrome. Lamotrigine also acts as a mood stabilizer.
Alprazolam	Alprazolam, also known under the trade names Xanax, Xanor and Niravam, is a short-acting drug of the benzodiazepine class used to treat moderate to severe anxiety disorders, panic attacks, and is used as an adjunctive treatment for anxiety associated with moderate depression. It is also available in an extended-release form, Xanax XR, both of which are now available in generic form. Alprazolam possesses anxiolytic, sedative, hypnotic, anticonvulsant, and muscle relaxant properties.
Benzodiazepine	A Benzodiazepine is a psychoactive drug whose core chemical structure is the fusion of a benzene ring and a diazepine ring. Benzodiazepine s have varying sedative, hypnotic , anxiolytic (anti-anxiety), anticonvulsant, muscle relaxant and amnesic properties. These properties make Benzodiazepine s useful in treating anxiety, insomnia, agitation, seizures, muscle spasms, alcohol withdrawal and as a premedication for medical or dental procedures.
Clonazepam	Clonazepam is a benzodiazepine derivative with highly potent anticonvulsant, muscle relaxant, and anxiolytic properties. It is marketed by Roche under the trade-names Klonopin in the United States, and Ravotril in Chile. Other names like Rivotril or Rivatril are known throughout the large majority of the rest of the world.

Stroke	A Stroke is the rapidly developing loss of brain function(s) due to disturbance in the blood supply to the brain. This can be due to ischemia (lack of blood supply) caused by thrombosis or embolism or due to a hemorrhage. As a result, the affected area of the brain is unable to function, leading to inability to move one or more limbs on one side of the body, inability to understand or formulate speech, or inability to see one side of the visual field.
Pathophysiology	Pathophysiology is the study of the changes of normal mechanical, physical, and biochemical functions, either caused by a disease, or resulting from an abnormal syndrome. More formally, it is the branch of medicine which deals with any disturbances of body functions, caused by disease or prodromal symptoms. An alternate definition is "the study of the biological and physical manifestations of disease as they correlate with the underlying abnormalities and physiological disturbances." The study of pathology and the study of Pathophysiology often involves substantial overlap in diseases and processes, but pathology emphasizes direct observations, while Pathophysiology emphasizes quantifiable measurements.
Hydrocephalus	Hydrocephalus is a term derived from the Greek words "hydro" meaning water, and "cephalus" meaning head, and this condition is sometimes known as "water on the brain". People with Hydrocephalus have abnormal accumulation of cerebrospinal fluid in the ventricles, or cavities, of the brain. This may cause increased intracranial pressure inside the skull and progressive enlargement of the head, convulsion, and mental disability.
Leukemia	Leukemia is a cancer of the blood or bone marrow and is characterized by an abnormal proliferation (production by multiplication) of blood cells, usually white blood cells (leukocytes.) Leukemia is a broad term covering a spectrum of diseases. In turn, it is part of the even broader group of diseases called haematological neoplasms.
Seizure	An epileptic Seizure is a transient symptom of excessive or synchronous neuronal activity in the brain. It can manifest as an alteration in mental state, tonic or clonic movements, convulsions, and various other psychic symptoms (such as déjà vu or jamais vu.) The medical syndrome of recurrent, unprovoked Seizure s is termed epilepsy, but Seizure s can occur in people who do not have epilepsy.
Status epilepticus	Status epilepticus refers to a life-threatening condition in which the brain is in a state of persistent seizure. Definitions vary, but traditionally it is defined as one continuous unremitting seizure lasting longer than 30 minutes , or recurrent seizures without regaining consciousness between seizures for greater than 30 minutes. There is some evidence that 5 minutes is sufficient to damage neurons and that seizures are unlikely to self-terminate by that time.
Idiopathic	Idiopathic is an adjective used primarily in medicine meaning arising spontaneously or from an obscure or unknown cause. From Greek á¼´διος, idios + πÎ¬θος, pathos (suffering), it means approximately "a disease of its own kind." It is technically a term from nosology, the classification of disease. For most medical conditions, one or more causes are somewhat understood, but in a certain percentage of people with the condition, the cause may not be readily apparent or characterized.

Simple partial seizures	Simple partial seizures are seizures which affect only a small region of the brain, often the temporal lobes and/or hippocampi. People who have Simple partial seizures retain consciousness. Simple partial seizures are often precursors to larger seizures, where the abnormal electrical activity spreads to a larger area of (or all of) the brain, usually resulting in a complex partial seizure or a tonic-clonic seizure.
Juvenile myoclonic Epilepsy	Juvenile Myoclonic Epilepsy is an idiopathic generalized epileptic syndrome with distinctive clinical and EEG features. Prevalence is 8-10% among adult patients with seizures. Fifteen percent of children with childhood absence epilepsy later develop Juvenile Myoclonic Epilepsy. It also is more likely in people who have family members with generalized epilepsy.
Brain tumor	A Brain tumor is an abnormal growth of cells within the brain or inside the skull, which can be cancerous or non-cancerous (benign.) It is defined as any intracranial tumor created by abnormal and uncontrolled cell division, normally either in the brain itself (neurons, glial cells (astrocytes, oligodendrocytes, ependymal cells), lymphatic tissue, blood vessels), in the cranial nerves (myelin-producing Schwann cells), in the brain envelopes (meninges), skull, pituitary and pineal gland, or spread from cancers primarily located in other organs (metastatic tumors.) Primary (true) Brain tumor s are commonly located in the posterior cranial fossa in children and in the anterior two-thirds of the cerebral hemispheres in adults, although they can affect any part of the brain.
Moyamoya syndrome	Moyamoya syndrome is an inherited disease in which certain arteries in the brain are constricted. Blood flow is blocked by the constriction, and also by blood clots . The blood vessels develop collateral circulation around the blocked vessels to compensate for the blockage, but the collateral vessels are small, weak, and prone to hemorrhage, aneurysm and thrombosis.
Fibroepithelial neoplasms	Fibroepithelial neoplasms are biphasic tumors. This means they consist of epithelial tissue, and stromal or mesenchymal tissue. They may be benign or malignant.
Astrocytoma	Astrocytoma s are cancers of the brain that originate in star-shaped brain cells called astrocytes. They account for roughly 75% of neuroepithelial tumors. Of numerous grading systems in use, the most common is the World Health Organization (WHO) grading system for Astrocytoma
Retinitis pigmentosa	Retinitis pigmentosa is a group of genetic eye conditions. In the progression of symptoms for Retinitis pigmentosa, night blindness generally precedes tunnel vision by years or even decades. Many people with Retinitis pigmentosa do not become legally blind until their 40s or 50s and retain some sight all their lives .

Merozoite surface protein	A Merozoite surface protein is a protein molecule taken from the skin of a merozoite. A merozoite is a "daughter cell" of a protozoan. Merozoite surface protein s are useful in researching malaria, a disease caused by protozoans.
Chromophobe	The term Chromophobe refers to histological structures which do not take up colored dye readily, and thus appear more relatively pale under the microscope -- hence their "fear" ("phobia") of "color" ("chrome".) The term is most commonly associated with the anterior pituitary, where approximately half of the cells are considered Chromophobe s. (Of the remaining cells, about a third are basophils, and the other two thirds acidophils.)
Adenoma	An Adenoma is a benign tumor (-oma) of glandular origin. Adenoma s can grow from many organs including the colon, adrenal glands, pituitary gland, thyroid, etc. Although these growths are benign, over time they may progress to become malignant, at which point they are called adenocarcinomas.
Carcinoma	A Carcinoma is any malignant cancer that arises from epithelial cells. Carcinoma s invade surrounding tissues and organs and may metastasize, or spread, to lymph nodes and other sites.

Pathophysiology	Pathophysiology is the study of the changes of normal mechanical, physical, and biochemical functions, either caused by a disease, or resulting from an abnormal syndrome. More formally, it is the branch of medicine which deals with any disturbances of body functions, caused by disease or prodromal symptoms.
	An alternate definition is "the study of the biological and physical manifestations of disease as they correlate with the underlying abnormalities and physiological disturbances."
	The study of pathology and the study of Pathophysiology often involves substantial overlap in diseases and processes, but pathology emphasizes direct observations, while Pathophysiology emphasizes quantifiable measurements.
Diagnosis	In medicine, diagnosis is the process of identifying a medical condition or disease by its signs, symptoms, and from the results of various diagnostic procedures. The conclusion reached through this process is called a diagnosis. The term "diagnostic criteria" designates the combination of signs, symptoms, and test results that allows the doctor to ascertain the diagnosis of the respective disease.
Dysplasia	Dysplasia is a term used in pathology to refer to an abnormality in maturation of cells within a tissue. This generally consists of an expansion of immature cells, with a corresponding decrease in the number and location of mature cells. Dysplasia is often indicative of an early neoplastic process.
Adenoma	An Adenoma is a benign tumor (-oma) of glandular origin. Adenoma s can grow from many organs including the colon, adrenal glands, pituitary gland, thyroid, etc. Although these growths are benign, over time they may progress to become malignant, at which point they are called adenocarcinomas.
Primary	In medicine, the reporting of symptoms by a patient may have significant psychological motivators. Psychologists sometimes categorize these motivators into primary or secondary gain.
	primary gain is internally good; motivationally.
Carcinoma	A Carcinoma is any malignant cancer that arises from epithelial cells. Carcinoma s invade surrounding tissues and organs and may metastasize, or spread, to lymph nodes and other sites.
Glucose	Glucose, a monosaccharide also known as grape sugar, blood sugar is a very important carbohydrate in biology. The living cell uses it as a source of energy and metabolic intermediate. Glucose is one of the main products of photosynthesis and starts cellular respiration in both prokaryotes and eukaryotes
Glucose tolerance test	A Glucose tolerance test in medical practice is the administration of glucose to determine how quickly it is cleared from the blood. The test is usually used to test for diabetes, insulin resistance, and sometimes reactive hypoglycemia. The glucose is most often given orally so the common test is technically an oral Glucose tolerance test
Idiopathic	Idiopathic is an adjective used primarily in medicine meaning arising spontaneously or from an obscure or unknown cause. From Greek á¼´διος, idios + πῖ¬θος, pathos (suffering), it means approximately "a disease of its own kind."

It is technically a term from nosology, the classification of disease. For most medical conditions, one or more causes are somewhat understood, but in a certain percentage of people with the condition, the cause may not be readily apparent or characterized.

Stroke	A Stroke is the rapidly developing loss of brain function(s) due to disturbance in the blood supply to the brain. This can be due to ischemia (lack of blood supply) caused by thrombosis or embolism or due to a hemorrhage. As a result, the affected area of the brain is unable to function, leading to inability to move one or more limbs on one side of the body, inability to understand or formulate speech, or inability to see one side of the visual field.
Transferrin	Transferrin is a blood plasma protein for iron ion delivery that, in humans, is encoded by the TF gene. Transferrin is a glycoprotein that binds iron very tightly but reversibly. Although iron bound to Transferrin is less than 0.1% (4 mg) of the total body iron, it is the most important iron pool, with the highest rate of turnover (25 mg/24 h.)
Inflammation	Inflammation is the complex biological response of vascular tissues to harmful stimuli, such as pathogens, damaged cells, or irritants. It is a protective attempt by the organism to remove the injurious stimuli as well as initiate the healing process for the tissue. Inflammation is not a synonym for infection.
Polyol pathway	Also called the sorbitol-aldose reductase pathway, the Polyol pathway appears to be implicated in diabetic complications, especially in microvascular damage to the retina, kidney, and nerves. Cells use glucose for energy, though unused glucose enters the Polyol pathway when aldose reductase reduces it to sorbitol. This reaction oxidizes NADPH to NADP+.
Etiology	Etiology is the study of causation, or origination. The word is most commonly used in medical and philosophical theories, where it is used to refer to the study of why things occur, or even the reasons behind the way that things act, and is used in philosophy, physics, psychology, government, medicine, theology and biology in reference to the causes of various phenomena. An etiological myth is a myth intended to explain a name or create a mythic history for a place or family.
Diabetic retinopathy	Diabetic retinopathy is retinopathy (damage to the retina) caused by complications of diabetes mellitus, which can eventually lead to blindness. It is an ocular manifestation of systemic disease which affects up to 80% of all patients who have had diabetes for 10 years or more. Despite these intimidating statistics, research indicates that at least 90% of these new cases could be reduced if there was proper and vigilant treatment and monitoring of the eyes.
Microangiopathy	Microangiopathy is an angiopathy affecting small blood vessels in the body. It can be contrasted to macroangiopathy. This sometimes occurs when a person has had diabetes mellitus for a long time.

Atypia	Atypia is a clinical term for abnormality in a cell. The term is medical jargon for an atypical cell. It may or may not be a precancerous indication associated with later malignancy, but the level of appropriate concern is highly dependent on the context with which it is diagnosed.
Lesion	A Lesion is any abnormal tissue found on or in an organism, usually damaged by disease or trauma. Lesion is derived from the Latin word laesio which means injury. Lesion s are caused by any process that damages tissues.
Gingivitis	Gingivitis around the teeth is a general term for gingival diseases affecting the gingiva As generally used, the term Gingivitis refers to gingival inflammation induced by bacterial biofilms adherent to tooth surfaces. Gingivitis can be defined as inflammation of the gingival tissue without loss of tooth attachment
Blood test	A Blood test is a laboratory analysis performed on a blood sample that is usually extracted from a vein in the arm using a needle, or via fingerprick. Blood test s are used to determine physiological and biochemical states, such as disease, mineral content, drug effectiveness, and organ function. Although the term Blood test is used, most routine tests (except for most haematology) are done on plasma or serum, instead of blood cells.
Cancer	Cancer is a class of diseases in which a group of cells display uncontrolled growth (division beyond the normal limits), invasion (intrusion on and destruction of adjacent tissues), and sometimes metastasis (spread to other locations in the body via lymph or blood.) These three malignant properties of cancers differentiate them from benign tumors, which are self-limited, and do not invade or metastasize. Most cancers form a tumor but some, like leukemia, do not.

Idiopathic	Idiopathic is an adjective used primarily in medicine meaning arising spontaneously or from an obscure or unknown cause. From Greek á¼´διος, idios + πῖ¬θος, pathos (suffering), it means approximately "a disease of its own kind."
	It is technically a term from nosology, the classification of disease. For most medical conditions, one or more causes are somewhat understood, but in a certain percentage of people with the condition, the cause may not be readily apparent or characterized.
Pathophysiology	Pathophysiology is the study of the changes of normal mechanical, physical, and biochemical functions, either caused by a disease, or resulting from an abnormal syndrome. More formally, it is the branch of medicine which deals with any disturbances of body functions, caused by disease or prodromal symptoms.
	An alternate definition is "the study of the biological and physical manifestations of disease as they correlate with the underlying abnormalities and physiological disturbances."
	The study of pathology and the study of Pathophysiology often involves substantial overlap in diseases and processes, but pathology emphasizes direct observations, while Pathophysiology emphasizes quantifiable measurements.
Neoplasm	Neoplasm is an abnormal mass of tissue as a result of neoplasia. Neoplasia is the abnormal proliferation of cells. The growth of this clone of cells exceeds, and is uncoordinated with, that of the normal tissues around it.
Cancer	Cancer is a class of diseases in which a group of cells display uncontrolled growth (division beyond the normal limits), invasion (intrusion on and destruction of adjacent tissues), and sometimes metastasis (spread to other locations in the body via lymph or blood.) These three malignant properties of cancers differentiate them from benign tumors, which are self-limited, and do not invade or metastasize. Most cancers form a tumor but some, like leukemia, do not.
Lewy bodies	Lewy bodies are abnormal aggregates of protein that develop inside nerve cells. They are identified under the microscope when histology is performed on the brain.
	Lewy bodies appear as spherical masses that displace other cell components.
Primary	In medicine, the reporting of symptoms by a patient may have significant psychological motivators. Psychologists sometimes categorize these motivators into primary or secondary gain.
	primary gain is internally good; motivationally.
Lymphatic system	The Lymphatic system in vertebrates is a network of conduits that carry a clear fluid called lymph. It also includes the lymphoid tissue through which the lymph travels. Lymphoid tissue is found in many organs, particularly the lymph nodes, and in the lymphoid follicles associated with the digestive system such as the tonsils.
Sarcoma	A Sarcoma is a cancer of the connective tissue resulting in mesoderm proliferation.
	This is in contrast to carcinomas, which are of epithelial origin (breast, colon, pancreas, and others.) However, due to an evolving understanding of tissue origin, the term "Sarcoma" is sometimes applied to tumors now known to arise from epithelial tissue.

Venereal Disease Research Laboratory test	The Venereal Disease Research Laboratory test or VDRL was developed by the former Venereal Disease Research Laboratory, now the Treponemal Pathogenesis and Immunology Branch, of the United States Public Health Service. The VDRL type test was invented before World War I, with its first iteration being that developed by August Paul von Wasserman with the aid of Albert Neisser in 1906. The VDRL test, as it is largely still done today, was developed in 1946 by Harris, Rosenberg, and Riedel.
Biopsy	A Biopsy is a medical test involving the removal of cells or tissues for examination. It is the removal of tissue from a living subject to determine the presence or extent of a disease. The tissue is generally examined under a microscope by a pathologist, and can also be analyzed chemically.
Blood test	A Blood test is a laboratory analysis performed on a blood sample that is usually extracted from a vein in the arm using a needle, or via fingerprick. Blood test s are used to determine physiological and biochemical states, such as disease, mineral content, drug effectiveness, and organ function. Although the term Blood test is used, most routine tests (except for most haematology) are done on plasma or serum, instead of blood cells.

Dysplasia	Dysplasia is a term used in pathology to refer to an abnormality in maturation of cells within a tissue. This generally consists of an expansion of immature cells, with a corresponding decrease in the number and location of mature cells. Dysplasia is often indicative of an early neoplastic process.
Primary	In medicine, the reporting of symptoms by a patient may have significant psychological motivators. Psychologists sometimes categorize these motivators into primary or secondary gain. primary gain is internally good; motivationally.
Diagnosis	In medicine, diagnosis is the process of identifying a medical condition or disease by its signs, symptoms, and from the results of various diagnostic procedures. The conclusion reached through this process is called a diagnosis. The term "diagnostic criteria" designates the combination of signs, symptoms, and test results that allows the doctor to ascertain the diagnosis of the respective disease.
Intracranial hemorrhage	An Intracranial hemorrhage is a hemorrhage within the skull. Intracranial bleeding occurs when a blood vessel within the skull is ruptured or leaks. It can result from physical trauma (as occurs in head injury) or nontraumatic causes (as occurs in hemorrhagic stroke) such as a ruptured aneurysm.
Cancer	Cancer is a class of diseases in which a group of cells display uncontrolled growth (division beyond the normal limits), invasion (intrusion on and destruction of adjacent tissues), and sometimes metastasis (spread to other locations in the body via lymph or blood.) These three malignant properties of cancers differentiate them from benign tumors, which are self-limited, and do not invade or metastasize. Most cancers form a tumor but some, like leukemia, do not.
Pathophysiology	Pathophysiology is the study of the changes of normal mechanical, physical, and biochemical functions, either caused by a disease, or resulting from an abnormal syndrome. More formally, it is the branch of medicine which deals with any disturbances of body functions, caused by disease or prodromal symptoms. An alternate definition is "the study of the biological and physical manifestations of disease as they correlate with the underlying abnormalities and physiological disturbances." The study of pathology and the study of Pathophysiology often involves substantial overlap in diseases and processes, but pathology emphasizes direct observations, while Pathophysiology emphasizes quantifiable measurements.
Sarcoma	A Sarcoma is a cancer of the connective tissue resulting in mesoderm proliferation. This is in contrast to carcinomas, which are of epithelial origin (breast, colon, pancreas, and others.) However, due to an evolving understanding of tissue origin, the term "Sarcoma" is sometimes applied to tumors now known to arise from epithelial tissue.
Idiopathic	Idiopathic is an adjective used primarily in medicine meaning arising spontaneously or from an obscure or unknown cause. From Greek á¼´διος, idios + πῖ¬θος, pathos (suffering), it means approximately "a disease of its own kind."

It is technically a term from nosology, the classification of disease. For most medical conditions, one or more causes are somewhat understood, but in a certain percentage of people with the condition, the cause may not be readily apparent or characterized.

Inflammation	Inflammation is the complex biological response of vascular tissues to harmful stimuli, such as pathogens, damaged cells, or irritants. It is a protective attempt by the organism to remove the injurious stimuli as well as initiate the healing process for the tissue. Inflammation is not a synonym for infection.
Neoplasm	Neoplasm is an abnormal mass of tissue as a result of neoplasia. Neoplasia is the abnormal proliferation of cells. The growth of this clone of cells exceeds, and is uncoordinated with, that of the normal tissues around it.
Atypia	Atypia is a clinical term for abnormality in a cell. The term is medical jargon for an atypical cell. It may or may not be a precancerous indication associated with later malignancy, but the level of appropriate concern is highly dependent on the context with which it is diagnosed.
Lesion	A Lesion is any abnormal tissue found on or in an organism, usually damaged by disease or trauma. Lesion is derived from the Latin word laesio which means injury. Lesion s are caused by any process that damages tissues.
Endometrial polyp	An Endometrial polyp or uterine polyp is a sessile mass in the inner lining of the uterus. They may have a large flat base (sessile) or be attached to the uterus by an elongated pedicle (pedunculated.) Pedunculated polyps are more common than sessile ones.
Leiomyoma	A Leiomyoma (plural is " Leiomyoma ta") is a benign smooth muscle neoplasm that is not premalignant. They can occur in any organ, but the most common forms occur in the uterus, small bowel and the esophagus. · Greek: · leios = smooth · muV = mouse or muscle · oma = tumor · Latin: · Fibra = fiber Leiomyoma enucleated from a uterus. External surface on left; cut surface on right Uterine fibroids are Leiomyoma ta of the uterine smooth muscle.
Carcinoma	A Carcinoma is any malignant cancer that arises from epithelial cells. Carcinoma s invade surrounding tissues and organs and may metastasize, or spread, to lymph nodes and other sites.

High-grade prostatic intraepithelial neoplasia	In urologic pathology, High-grade prostatic intraepithelial neoplasia, abbreviated HGPIN, is an abnormality of prostatic glands and believed to precede the development of prostate adenocarcinoma (the most common form of prostate cancer.) It is considered to be a pre-malignancy of the prostatic glands. On a subsequent biopsy, given a history of a HGPIN diagnosis, the chance of finding prostatic adenocarcinoma is approximately 30%.
Pathogenesis	The term Pathogenesis means step by step development of a disease and the chain of events leading to that disease due to a series of changes in the structure and /or function of a cell/tissue/organ being caused by a microbial, chemical or physical agent. The Pathogenesis of a disease is the mechanism by which an etiological factor causes the disease. The term can also be used to describe the development of the disease, such as acute, chronic and recurrent.
Metaplasia	Metaplasia is the reversible replacement of one differentiated cell type with another mature differentiated cell type. The change from one type of cell to another is generally caused by some sort of abnormal stimulus. In simplistic terms, it is as if the original cells are not robust enough to withstand the new environment, and so they change into another type more suited to the new environment.
Ferritin	Ferritin is a globular protein complex consisting of 24 protein subunits and is the primary intracellular iron-storage protein in both prokaryotes and eukaryotes, keeping iron in a soluble and non-toxic form. Ferritin that is not combined with iron is called apo Ferritin .
Hyperplasia	Hyperplasia is a general term referring to the proliferation of cells within an organ or tissue beyond that which is ordinarily seen (e.g. constantly dividing cells.) Hyperplasia may result in the gross enlargement of an organ, the formation of a benign tumor, or may be visible only under a microscope. Hyperplasia is different from hypertrophy in that the adaptive cell change in hypertrophy is by increased cellular size only, whereas in Hyperplasia it is by increased cellular number.
Hypertrophy	Hypertrophy is the increase in the volume of an organ or tissue due to the enlargement of its component cells. It should be distinguished from hyperplasia, in which the cells remain approximately the same size but increase in number. Although Hypertrophy and hyperplasia are two distinct process, they frequently occur together, such as in the case of the hormonally-induced proliferation and enlargement of the cells of the uterus during pregnancy.
Fibroepithelial neoplasms	Fibroepithelial neoplasms are biphasic tumors. This means they consist of epithelial tissue, and stromal or mesenchymal tissue. They may be benign or malignant.
Lactate dehydrogenase	Lactate dehydrogenase (Lactate dehydrogenase H) is an enzyme (EC 1.1.1.27) present in a wide variety of organisms, including plants and animals. Lactate dehydrogenase s exist in four distinct enzyme classes. Two of them are cytochrome c-dependent enzymes with each acting on either D-lactate (EC 1.1.2.4) or L-lactate (EC 1.1.2.3.)

Breast cyst	A Breast cyst is a fluid-filled sac within your breast. You can have one or many Breast cyst s. They"re often described as round or oval lumps with distinct edges.
Biopsy	A Biopsy is a medical test involving the removal of cells or tissues for examination. It is the removal of tissue from a living subject to determine the presence or extent of a disease. The tissue is generally examined under a microscope by a pathologist, and can also be analyzed chemically.
Carcinoembryonic antigen	Carcinoembryonic antigen is a glycoprotein involved in cell adhesion. It is normally produced during fetal development, but the production of CEA stops before birth. Therefore, it is not usually present in the blood of healthy adults, although levels are raised in heavy smokers.

Diagnosis	In medicine, diagnosis is the process of identifying a medical condition or disease by its signs, symptoms, and from the results of various diagnostic procedures. The conclusion reached through this process is called a diagnosis. The term "diagnostic criteria" designates the combination of signs, symptoms, and test results that allows the doctor to ascertain the diagnosis of the respective disease.
Etiology	Etiology is the study of causation, or origination.
	The word is most commonly used in medical and philosophical theories, where it is used to refer to the study of why things occur, or even the reasons behind the way that things act, and is used in philosophy, physics, psychology, government, medicine, theology and biology in reference to the causes of various phenomena. An etiological myth is a myth intended to explain a name or create a mythic history for a place or family.
Neoplasm	Neoplasm is an abnormal mass of tissue as a result of neoplasia. Neoplasia is the abnormal proliferation of cells. The growth of this clone of cells exceeds, and is uncoordinated with, that of the normal tissues around it.
Pathophysiology	Pathophysiology is the study of the changes of normal mechanical, physical, and biochemical functions, either caused by a disease, or resulting from an abnormal syndrome. More formally, it is the branch of medicine which deals with any disturbances of body functions, caused by disease or prodromal symptoms.
	An alternate definition is "the study of the biological and physical manifestations of disease as they correlate with the underlying abnormalities and physiological disturbances."
	The study of pathology and the study of Pathophysiology often involves substantial overlap in diseases and processes, but pathology emphasizes direct observations, while Pathophysiology emphasizes quantifiable measurements.
Cancer	Cancer is a class of diseases in which a group of cells display uncontrolled growth (division beyond the normal limits), invasion (intrusion on and destruction of adjacent tissues), and sometimes metastasis (spread to other locations in the body via lymph or blood.) These three malignant properties of cancers differentiate them from benign tumors, which are self-limited, and do not invade or metastasize. Most cancers form a tumor but some, like leukemia, do not.
Gumma	A Gumma is a soft, non-cancerous growth resulting from the tertiary stage of syphilis. It is a form of granuloma. Gummas are most commonly found in the liver (Gumma hepatis), but can also be found in brain, heart, skin, bone, testis, and other tissues, leading to a variety of potential problems including neurological disorders or heart valve disease.
Primary	In medicine, the reporting of symptoms by a patient may have significant psychological motivators. Psychologists sometimes categorize these motivators into primary or secondary gain.
	primary gain is internally good; motivationally.

Rapid plasma reagin	Rapid plasma reagin refers to a type of test that looks for non-specific antibodies in the blood of the patient that may indicate that the organism (Treponema pallidum) that causes syphilis is present. The term "reagin" means that this test does not look for antibodies against the actual bacterium, but rather for antibodies against substances released by cells when they are damaged by T. pallidum. Another test often used to screen for syphilis is the Venereal Disease Research Laboratory VDRL slide test.
Venereal Disease Research Laboratory test	The Venereal Disease Research Laboratory test or VDRL was developed by the former Venereal Disease Research Laboratory, now the Treponemal Pathogenesis and Immunology Branch, of the United States Public Health Service. The VDRL type test was invented before World War I, with its first iteration being that developed by August Paul von Wasserman with the aid of Albert Neisser in 1906. The VDRL test, as it is largely still done today, was developed in 1946 by Harris, Rosenberg, and Riedel.
Azithromycin	Azithromycin is an azalide, a subclass of macrolide antibiotics. Azithromycin is one of the world"s best-selling antibiotics, and is derived from erythromycin; however, it differs chemically from erythromycin in that a methyl-substituted nitrogen atom is incorporated into the lactone ring, thus making the lactone ring 15-membered. Azithromycin is used to treat or prevent certain bacterial infections, most often those causing middle ear infections, tonsillitis, throat infections, laryngitis, bronchitis, pneumonia, Typhoid, chlamydia, and sinusitis.
Granuloma	Granuloma is a medical term for a ball-like collection of immune cells which forms when the immune system attempts to wall off substances that it perceives as foreign but is unable to eliminate. Such substances include infectious organisms such as bacteria and fungi as well as other materials such as keratin, suture fragments and vegetable particles. A Granuloma is therefore a special type of inflammatory reaction that can occur in a wide variety of diseases, both infectious and non-infectious.
Doxycycline	Doxycycline is a member of the tetracycline antibiotics group and is commonly used to treat a variety of infections. Doxycycline is a semi-synthetic tetracycline invented and clinically developed in the early 1960s by Pfizer Inc. and marketed under the brand name Vibramycin.
Intracranial hemorrhage	An Intracranial hemorrhage is a hemorrhage within the skull. Intracranial bleeding occurs when a blood vessel within the skull is ruptured or leaks. It can result from physical trauma (as occurs in head injury) or nontraumatic causes (as occurs in hemorrhagic stroke) such as a ruptured aneurysm.
Lesion	A Lesion is any abnormal tissue found on or in an organism, usually damaged by disease or trauma. Lesion is derived from the Latin word laesio which means injury. Lesion s are caused by any process that damages tissues.

Lice	Lice, are an order of over 3,000 species of wingless insects; three of which are classified as human disease agents. They are obligate ectoparasites of every avian and most mammalian orders. They are not found on Monotremes and a few eutherian orders, namely the bats, whales, dolphins and porpoises and pangolins
Pediculosis	Pediculosis is an infestation of lice -- blood-feeding ectoparasitic insects of the order Phthiraptera. The condition can occur in almost any species of warm-blooded animal (i.e., mammals and birds), including humans. Although "Pediculosis" in humans may properly refer to lice infestation of any part of the body, the term is sometimes used loosely to refer to Pediculosis capitis, the infestation of the human head with the specific head louse.
Permethrin	Permethrin is a common synthetic chemical, widely used as an insecticide, acaricide, and insect repellent. It belongs to the family of synthetic chemicals called pyrethroids and functions as a neurotoxin, affecting neuron membranes by prolonging sodium channel activation. It is not known to rapidly harm most mammals or birds, but is highly toxic to fish and cats.
Entamoeba	Entamoeba is a genus of Amoebozoa found as internal parasites or commensals of animals. In 1875, Fedor Lösch described the first proven case of amoebic dysentery in St Petersburg, Russia. He referred to the amoeba he observed microscopically as "Amoeba coli"; however it is not clear whether he was using this as a descriptive term or intended it as a formal taxonomic name.
Entamoeba histolytica	Entamoeba histolytica is an anaerobic parasitic protozoan, part of the genus Entamoeba. Predominantly infecting humans and other primates, E. histolytica is estimated to infect about 50 million people worldwide. Many older textbooks state that 10% of the world population is infected, but these figures predate the recognition that at least 90% of these infections were due to a second species, E. dispar.
Giardia lamblia	Giardia lamblia is a flagellated protozoan parasite that colonises and reproduces in the small intestine, causing giardiasis. The giardia parasite attaches to the epithelium by a ventral adhesive disc, and reproduces via binary fission. Giardiasis does not spread via the bloodstream, nor does it spread to other parts of the gastro-intestinal tract, but remains confined to the lumen of the small intestine.
Giardiasis	Giardiasis in humans is caused by the infection of the small intestine by a single-celled organism called Giardia lamblia. Giardiasis occurs worldwide with a prevalence of 20-30% in developing countries. Additionally, Giardia has a wide range of human and other mammalian hosts, thus making it very difficult to eliminate.
Quinacrine	Quinacrine is a drug with a number of different medical applications. Quinacrine was initially approved in the 1930s as an antimalarial drug. This antiprotozoal is also approved for the the treatment of Giardiasis (an intestinal parasite), and has been researched as an inhibitor of phospholipase A2.

Trophozoite | A Trophozoite is the activated, feeding stage in the life cycle of protozoan parasites such as the malaria-causing Plasmodium falciparum (the opposite of the Trophozoite state is the thick-walled cyst form.) The Trophozoite undergoes schizogony (asexual reproduction) and develops into a schizont which contains merozoites. Another type of Balantidium coli is cysts.

Gingivitis	Gingivitis around the teeth is a general term for gingival diseases affecting the gingiva As generally used, the term Gingivitis refers to gingival inflammation induced by bacterial biofilms adherent to tooth surfaces.
	Gingivitis can be defined as inflammation of the gingival tissue without loss of tooth attachment
Pathogenesis	The term Pathogenesis means step by step development of a disease and the chain of events leading to that disease due to a series of changes in the structure and /or function of a cell/tissue/organ being caused by a microbial, chemical or physical agent. The Pathogenesis of a disease is the mechanism by which an etiological factor causes the disease. The term can also be used to describe the development of the disease, such as acute, chronic and recurrent.
Platelet	Platelet s are small, irregularly-shaped anuclear cells (i.e. cells that do not have a nucleus containing DNA), 2-4 µm in diameter, which are derived from fragmentation of precursor megakaryocytes. The average lifespan of a Platelet is between 8 and 12 days. Platelet s play a fundamental role in hemostasis and are a natural source of growth factors.
Carcinoma	A Carcinoma is any malignant cancer that arises from epithelial cells. Carcinoma s invade surrounding tissues and organs and may metastasize, or spread, to lymph nodes and other sites.
Seizure	An epileptic Seizure is a transient symptom of excessive or synchronous neuronal activity in the brain. It can manifest as an alteration in mental state, tonic or clonic movements, convulsions, and various other psychic symptoms (such as déjà vu or jamais vu.) The medical syndrome of recurrent, unprovoked Seizure s is termed epilepsy, but Seizure s can occur in people who do not have epilepsy.
Ferritin	Ferritin is a globular protein complex consisting of 24 protein subunits and is the primary intracellular iron-storage protein in both prokaryotes and eukaryotes, keeping iron in a soluble and non-toxic form. Ferritin that is not combined with iron is called apo Ferritin .
Bilirubin	Bilirubin is the yellow breakdown product of normal heme catabolism. Heme is found in hemoglobin, a principal component of red blood cells. Bilirubin is excreted in bile, and its levels are elevated in certain diseases.
Cancer	Cancer is a class of diseases in which a group of cells display uncontrolled growth (division beyond the normal limits), invasion (intrusion on and destruction of adjacent tissues), and sometimes metastasis (spread to other locations in the body via lymph or blood.) These three malignant properties of cancers differentiate them from benign tumors, which are self-limited, and do not invade or metastasize. Most cancers form a tumor but some, like leukemia, do not.

Hyperplasia	Hyperplasia is a general term referring to the proliferation of cells within an organ or tissue beyond that which is ordinarily seen (e.g. constantly dividing cells.) Hyperplasia may result in the gross enlargement of an organ, the formation of a benign tumor, or may be visible only under a microscope. Hyperplasia is different from hypertrophy in that the adaptive cell change in hypertrophy is by increased cellular size only, whereas in Hyperplasia it is by increased cellular number.
Inflammation	Inflammation is the complex biological response of vascular tissues to harmful stimuli, such as pathogens, damaged cells, or irritants. It is a protective attempt by the organism to remove the injurious stimuli as well as initiate the healing process for the tissue. Inflammation is not a synonym for infection.
Biopsy	A Biopsy is a medical test involving the removal of cells or tissues for examination. It is the removal of tissue from a living subject to determine the presence or extent of a disease. The tissue is generally examined under a microscope by a pathologist, and can also be analyzed chemically.
Blood test	A Blood test is a laboratory analysis performed on a blood sample that is usually extracted from a vein in the arm using a needle, or via fingerprick. Blood test s are used to determine physiological and biochemical states, such as disease, mineral content, drug effectiveness, and organ function. Although the term Blood test is used, most routine tests (except for most haematology) are done on plasma or serum, instead of blood cells.

Seizure	An epileptic Seizure is a transient symptom of excessive or synchronous neuronal activity in the brain. It can manifest as an alteration in mental state, tonic or clonic movements, convulsions, and various other psychic symptoms (such as déjà vu or jamais vu.) The medical syndrome of recurrent, unprovoked Seizure s is termed epilepsy, but Seizure s can occur in people who do not have epilepsy.
Leukemia	Leukemia is a cancer of the blood or bone marrow and is characterized by an abnormal proliferation (production by multiplication) of blood cells, usually white blood cells (leukocytes.) Leukemia is a broad term covering a spectrum of diseases. In turn, it is part of the even broader group of diseases called haematological neoplasms.
Pathophysiology	Pathophysiology is the study of the changes of normal mechanical, physical, and biochemical functions, either caused by a disease, or resulting from an abnormal syndrome. More formally, it is the branch of medicine which deals with any disturbances of body functions, caused by disease or prodromal symptoms. An alternate definition is "the study of the biological and physical manifestations of disease as they correlate with the underlying abnormalities and physiological disturbances." The study of pathology and the study of Pathophysiology often involves substantial overlap in diseases and processes, but pathology emphasizes direct observations, while Pathophysiology emphasizes quantifiable measurements.
Cancer	Cancer is a class of diseases in which a group of cells display uncontrolled growth (division beyond the normal limits), invasion (intrusion on and destruction of adjacent tissues), and sometimes metastasis (spread to other locations in the body via lymph or blood.) These three malignant properties of cancers differentiate them from benign tumors, which are self-limited, and do not invade or metastasize. Most cancers form a tumor but some, like leukemia, do not.
Glossitis	Glossitis is inflammation or infection of the tongue. It causes the tongue to swell and change color. Finger-like projections on the surface of the tongue (papillae) may be lost, causing the tongue to appear smooth.
Stomatitis	Stomatitis is an inflammation of the mucous lining of any of the structures in the mouth, which may involve the cheeks, gums, tongue, lips, throat, and roof or floor of the mouth. The inflammation can be caused by conditions in the mouth itself, such as poor oral hygiene, poorly fitted dentures, or from mouth burns from hot food or drinks, or by conditions that affect the entire body, such as medications, allergic reactions, radiation therapy, or infections. Severe iron deficiency anemia can lead to Stomatitis.
Colchicine	Colchicine is a toxic natural product and secondary metabolite, originally extracted from plants of the genus Colchicum Originally used to treat rheumatic complaints and especially gout and still finds use for these purposes today, it was also prescribed for its cathartic and emetic effects. Its present medicinal use is mainly in the treatment of gout; as well, it is being investigated for its potential use as an anti-cancer drug.

Hemolysin	Hemolysin s are exotoxins produced by bacteria which cause lysis of red blood cells in vitro. Visualization of hemolysis of red blood cells in agar plates facilitates the categorization of some pathogenic bacteria such as Streptococcus. Although the lytic activity of some Hemolysin s on red blood cells may be important for nutrient acquisition or for causing certain conditions such as anemia, many Hemolysin producing pathogens do not cause significant lysis of red blood cells during infection.
Hyperplasia	Hyperplasia is a general term referring to the proliferation of cells within an organ or tissue beyond that which is ordinarily seen (e.g. constantly dividing cells.) Hyperplasia may result in the gross enlargement of an organ, the formation of a benign tumor, or may be visible only under a microscope. Hyperplasia is different from hypertrophy in that the adaptive cell change in hypertrophy is by increased cellular size only, whereas in Hyperplasia it is by increased cellular number.

Neoplasm	Neoplasm is an abnormal mass of tissue as a result of neoplasia. Neoplasia is the abnormal proliferation of cells. The growth of this clone of cells exceeds, and is uncoordinated with, that of the normal tissues around it.
Leukemia	Leukemia is a cancer of the blood or bone marrow and is characterized by an abnormal proliferation (production by multiplication) of blood cells, usually white blood cells (leukocytes.) Leukemia is a broad term covering a spectrum of diseases. In turn, it is part of the even broader group of diseases called haematological neoplasms.
Pathophysiology	Pathophysiology is the study of the changes of normal mechanical, physical, and biochemical functions, either caused by a disease, or resulting from an abnormal syndrome. More formally, it is the branch of medicine which deals with any disturbances of body functions, caused by disease or prodromal symptoms. An alternate definition is "the study of the biological and physical manifestations of disease as they correlate with the underlying abnormalities and physiological disturbances." The study of pathology and the study of Pathophysiology often involves substantial overlap in diseases and processes, but pathology emphasizes direct observations, while Pathophysiology emphasizes quantifiable measurements.
Pathogenesis	The term Pathogenesis means step by step development of a disease and the chain of events leading to that disease due to a series of changes in the structure and /or function of a cell/tissue/organ being caused by a microbial, chemical or physical agent. The Pathogenesis of a disease is the mechanism by which an etiological factor causes the disease. The term can also be used to describe the development of the disease, such as acute, chronic and recurrent.
Rapid plasma reagin	Rapid plasma reagin refers to a type of test that looks for non-specific antibodies in the blood of the patient that may indicate that the organism (Treponema pallidum) that causes syphilis is present. The term "reagin" means that this test does not look for antibodies against the actual bacterium, but rather for antibodies against substances released by cells when they are damaged by T. pallidum. Another test often used to screen for syphilis is the Venereal Disease Research Laboratory VDRL slide test.
Fibroepithelial neoplasms	Fibroepithelial neoplasms are biphasic tumors. This means they consist of epithelial tissue, and stromal or mesenchymal tissue. They may be benign or malignant.
Lesion	A Lesion is any abnormal tissue found on or in an organism, usually damaged by disease or trauma. Lesion is derived from the Latin word laesio which means injury. Lesion s are caused by any process that damages tissues.
Ann Arbor staging	Ann Arbor staging is the staging system for lymphomas, both in Hodgkin"s lymphoma (previously called Hodgkin"s Disease) and Non-Hodgkin lymphoma It was initially developed for Hodgkin"s, but has some use in NHL. It has roughly the same function as TNM staging in solid tumors. The stage depends on both the place where the malignant tissue is located (as located with biopsy, CT scanning and increasingly positron emission tomography) and on systemic symptoms due to the lymphoma ("B symptoms": night sweats, weight loss of >10% or fevers.)

Platelet

Platelet s are small, irregularly-shaped anuclear cells (i.e. cells that do not have a nucleus containing DNA), 2-4 µm in diameter, which are derived from fragmentation of precursor megakaryocytes. The average lifespan of a Platelet is between 8 and 12 days. Platelet s play a fundamental role in hemostasis and are a natural source of growth factors.

Idiopathic

Idiopathic is an adjective used primarily in medicine meaning arising spontaneously or from an obscure or unknown cause. From Greek á¼´διος, idios + πÎ¬θος, pathos (suffering), it means approximately "a disease of its own kind."

It is technically a term from nosology, the classification of disease. For most medical conditions, one or more causes are somewhat understood, but in a certain percentage of people with the condition, the cause may not be readily apparent or characterized.

Cancer

Cancer is a class of diseases in which a group of cells display uncontrolled growth (division beyond the normal limits), invasion (intrusion on and destruction of adjacent tissues), and sometimes metastasis (spread to other locations in the body via lymph or blood.) These three malignant properties of cancers differentiate them from benign tumors, which are self-limited, and do not invade or metastasize. Most cancers form a tumor but some, like leukemia, do not.

Diagnosis

In medicine, diagnosis is the process of identifying a medical condition or disease by its signs, symptoms, and from the results of various diagnostic procedures. The conclusion reached through this process is called a diagnosis. The term "diagnostic criteria" designates the combination of signs, symptoms, and test results that allows the doctor to ascertain the diagnosis of the respective disease.

Platelet	Platelet s are small, irregularly-shaped anuclear cells (i.e. cells that do not have a nucleus containing DNA), 2-4 µm in diameter, which are derived from fragmentation of precursor megakaryocytes. The average lifespan of a Platelet is between 8 and 12 days. Platelet s play a fundamental role in hemostasis and are a natural source of growth factors.
Seizure	An epileptic Seizure is a transient symptom of excessive or synchronous neuronal activity in the brain. It can manifest as an alteration in mental state, tonic or clonic movements, convulsions, and various other psychic symptoms (such as déjà vu or jamais vu.) The medical syndrome of recurrent, unprovoked Seizure s is termed epilepsy, but Seizure s can occur in people who do not have epilepsy.
Hemolytic disease of the newborn	Hemolytic disease of the newborn HDN, HDFN is an alloimmune condition that develops in a fetus, when the IgG molecules that have been produced by the mother and have passed through the placenta include ones which attack the red blood cells in the fetal circulation. The red cells are broken down and the fetus can develop reticulocytosis and anaemia. This fetal disease ranges from mild to very severe, and fetal death from heart failure can occur.
Rh disease	Rh disease disease, Rhesus disease, RhD Hemolytic Disease of the Newborn, Rhesus D Hemolytic Disease of the Newborn or RhD HDN) is one of the causes of hemolytic disease of the newborn The disease ranges from mild to severe. When the disease is mild the fetus may have mild anaemia with reticulocytosis.
Pathophysiology	Pathophysiology is the study of the changes of normal mechanical, physical, and biochemical functions, either caused by a disease, or resulting from an abnormal syndrome. More formally, it is the branch of medicine which deals with any disturbances of body functions, caused by disease or prodromal symptoms. An alternate definition is "the study of the biological and physical manifestations of disease as they correlate with the underlying abnormalities and physiological disturbances." The study of pathology and the study of Pathophysiology often involves substantial overlap in diseases and processes, but pathology emphasizes direct observations, while Pathophysiology emphasizes quantifiable measurements.
Diagnosis	In medicine, diagnosis is the process of identifying a medical condition or disease by its signs, symptoms, and from the results of various diagnostic procedures. The conclusion reached through this process is called a diagnosis. The term "diagnostic criteria" designates the combination of signs, symptoms, and test results that allows the doctor to ascertain the diagnosis of the respective disease.
Blood transfusion	Blood transfusion is the process of transferring blood or blood-based products from one person into the circulatory system of another. Blood transfusion s can be life-saving in some situations, such as massive blood loss due to trauma, or can be used to replace blood lost during surgery. Blood transfusion s may also be used to treat a severe anaemia or thrombocytopenia caused by a blood disease.

Prothrombin time	The Prothrombin time and its derived measures of prothrombin ratio (PR) and international normalized ratio (INR) are measures of the extrinsic pathway of coagulation. They are used to determine the clotting tendency of blood, in the measure of warfarin dosage, liver damage, and vitamin K status. The reference range for Prothrombin time is usually around 12-15 seconds; the normal range for the INR is 0.8-1.2.
Thrombin time	The Thrombin time , is a blood test which measures the time it takes for a clot to form in the plasma from a blood sample in anticoagulant which had added an excess of thrombin,. This test is repeated with pooled plasma from normal patients. The difference in time between the test and the "normal" indicates an abnormality in the conversion of fibrinogen(a soluble protien) to fibrin an insoluble protien.
Partial thromboplastin time	The Partial thromboplastin time or activated Partial thromboplastin time is a performance indicator measuring the efficacy of both the "intrinsic" (now referred to as the contact activation pathway) and the common coagulation pathways. Apart from detecting abnormalities in blood clotting, it is also used to monitor the treatment effects with heparin, a major anticoagulant. It is used in conjunction with the prothrombin time (PT) which measures the extrinsic pathway.
Idiopathic	Idiopathic is an adjective used primarily in medicine meaning arising spontaneously or from an obscure or unknown cause. From Greek á¼´διος, idios + πῖ¬θος, pathos (suffering), it means approximately "a disease of its own kind." It is technically a term from nosology, the classification of disease. For most medical conditions, one or more causes are somewhat understood, but in a certain percentage of people with the condition, the cause may not be readily apparent or characterized.
Leukemia	Leukemia is a cancer of the blood or bone marrow and is characterized by an abnormal proliferation (production by multiplication) of blood cells, usually white blood cells (leukocytes.) Leukemia is a broad term covering a spectrum of diseases. In turn, it is part of the even broader group of diseases called haematological neoplasms.
Pathogenesis	The term Pathogenesis means step by step development of a disease and the chain of events leading to that disease due to a series of changes in the structure and /or function of a cell/tissue/organ being caused by a microbial, chemical or physical agent. The Pathogenesis of a disease is the mechanism by which an etiological factor causes the disease. The term can also be used to describe the development of the disease, such as acute, chronic and recurrent.
Ann Arbor staging	Ann Arbor staging is the staging system for lymphomas, both in Hodgkin"s lymphoma (previously called Hodgkin"s Disease) and Non-Hodgkin lymphoma It was initially developed for Hodgkin"s, but has some use in NHL. It has roughly the same function as TNM staging in solid tumors. The stage depends on both the place where the malignant tissue is located (as located with biopsy, CT scanning and increasingly positron emission tomography) and on systemic symptoms due to the lymphoma ("B symptoms": night sweats, weight loss of >10% or fevers.)

Carcinoma	A Carcinoma is any malignant cancer that arises from epithelial cells. Carcinoma s invade surrounding tissues and organs and may metastasize, or spread, to lymph nodes and other sites.
Stroke	A Stroke is the rapidly developing loss of brain function(s) due to disturbance in the blood supply to the brain. This can be due to ischemia (lack of blood supply) caused by thrombosis or embolism or due to a hemorrhage. As a result, the affected area of the brain is unable to function, leading to inability to move one or more limbs on one side of the body, inability to understand or formulate speech, or inability to see one side of the visual field.
Hyperplasia	Hyperplasia is a general term referring to the proliferation of cells within an organ or tissue beyond that which is ordinarily seen (e.g. constantly dividing cells.) Hyperplasia may result in the gross enlargement of an organ, the formation of a benign tumor, or may be visible only under a microscope. Hyperplasia is different from hypertrophy in that the adaptive cell change in hypertrophy is by increased cellular size only, whereas in Hyperplasia it is by increased cellular number.
Hypertrophy	Hypertrophy is the increase in the volume of an organ or tissue due to the enlargement of its component cells. It should be distinguished from hyperplasia, in which the cells remain approximately the same size but increase in number. Although Hypertrophy and hyperplasia are two distinct process, they frequently occur together, such as in the case of the hormonally-induced proliferation and enlargement of the cells of the uterus during pregnancy.
Fibroepithelial neoplasms	Fibroepithelial neoplasms are biphasic tumors. This means they consist of epithelial tissue, and stromal or mesenchymal tissue. They may be benign or malignant.
Transferrin	Transferrin is a blood plasma protein for iron ion delivery that, in humans, is encoded by the TF gene. Transferrin is a glycoprotein that binds iron very tightly but reversibly. Although iron bound to Transferrin is less than 0.1% (4 mg) of the total body iron, it is the most important iron pool, with the highest rate of turnover (25 mg/24 h.)
Lymphatic system	The Lymphatic system in vertebrates is a network of conduits that carry a clear fluid called lymph. It also includes the lymphoid tissue through which the lymph travels. Lymphoid tissue is found in many organs, particularly the lymph nodes, and in the lymphoid follicles associated with the digestive system such as the tonsils.
Blood test	A Blood test is a laboratory analysis performed on a blood sample that is usually extracted from a vein in the arm using a needle, or via fingerprick. Blood test s are used to determine physiological and biochemical states, such as disease, mineral content, drug effectiveness, and organ function. Although the term Blood test is used, most routine tests (except for most haematology) are done on plasma or serum, instead of blood cells.
Stenosis	A Stenosis is an abnormal narrowing in a blood vessel or other tubular organ or structure. It is also sometimes called a "stricture" (as in urethral stricture.) The term "coarctation" is synonymous, but is commonly used only in the context of aortic coarctation.

Aneurysm

An Aneurysm (or aneurism) is a localized, blood-filled dilation of a blood vessel caused by disease or weakening of the vessel wall.

Aneurysm s most commonly occur in arteries at the base of the brain (the circle of Willis) and in the aorta (the main artery coming out of the heart, a so-called aortic Aneurysm) As the size of an Aneurysm increases, there is an increased risk of rupture, which can result in severe hemorrhage or other complications including sudden death.

Gingivitis	Gingivitis around the teeth is a general term for gingival diseases affecting the gingiva As generally used, the term Gingivitis refers to gingival inflammation induced by bacterial biofilms adherent to tooth surfaces. Gingivitis can be defined as inflammation of the gingival tissue without loss of tooth attachment
Pathophysiology	Pathophysiology is the study of the changes of normal mechanical, physical, and biochemical functions, either caused by a disease, or resulting from an abnormal syndrome. More formally, it is the branch of medicine which deals with any disturbances of body functions, caused by disease or prodromal symptoms. An alternate definition is "the study of the biological and physical manifestations of disease as they correlate with the underlying abnormalities and physiological disturbances." The study of pathology and the study of Pathophysiology often involves substantial overlap in diseases and processes, but pathology emphasizes direct observations, while Pathophysiology emphasizes quantifiable measurements.
Platelet	Platelet s are small, irregularly-shaped anuclear cells (i.e. cells that do not have a nucleus containing DNA), 2-4 µm in diameter, which are derived from fragmentation of precursor megakaryocytes. The average lifespan of a Platelet is between 8 and 12 days. Platelet s play a fundamental role in hemostasis and are a natural source of growth factors.
Fibroepithelial neoplasms	Fibroepithelial neoplasms are biphasic tumors. This means they consist of epithelial tissue, and stromal or mesenchymal tissue. They may be benign or malignant.
Aneurysm	An Aneurysm (or aneurism) is a localized, blood-filled dilation of a blood vessel caused by disease or weakening of the vessel wall. Aneurysm s most commonly occur in arteries at the base of the brain (the circle of Willis) and in the aorta (the main artery coming out of the heart, a so-called aortic Aneurysm) As the size of an Aneurysm increases, there is an increased risk of rupture, which can result in severe hemorrhage or other complications including sudden death.
Pseudoaneurysm	A Pseudoaneurysm is an hematoma that forms as the result of a leaking hole in an artery. Note that the hematoma forms outside the arterial wall, so it is contained by the surrounding tissues. Also it must continue to communicate with the artery to be considered a Pseudoaneurysm.
Hematoma	A Hematoma is a collection of blood outside the blood vessels, generally the result of hemorrhage internal bleeding. It is not to be confused with hemangioma which is an abnormal build up of blood vessels in the skin or internal organs. Hematoma - from Greek αῖμα, haima, blood + τωμα, t-oma, indicating an abnormality.
Infarction	In medicine, an Infarction is the process of tissue death (necrosis) caused by blockage of the tissue"s blood supply. The supplying artery may be blocked by an obstruction (e.g. an embolus, thrombus, or atherosclerotic plaque), may be mechanically compressed (e.g. tumor, volvulus, or hernia), ruptured by trauma (e.g. atherosclerosis or vasculitides), or vasoconstricted (e.g. cocaine vasoconstriction leading to myocardial Infarction)

Infarction s are commonly associated with hypertension or atherosclerosis.

C-reactive protein	C-reactive protein is a protein found in the blood, the levels of which rise in response to inflammation (an acute-phase protein.) CRP is synthesized by the liver in response to factors released by fat cells (adipocytes.) It is a member of the pentraxin family of proteins.
Leukemia	Leukemia is a cancer of the blood or bone marrow and is characterized by an abnormal proliferation (production by multiplication) of blood cells, usually white blood cells (leukocytes.) Leukemia is a broad term covering a spectrum of diseases. In turn, it is part of the even broader group of diseases called haematological neoplasms.
Pathogenesis	The term Pathogenesis means step by step development of a disease and the chain of events leading to that disease due to a series of changes in the structure and /or function of a cell/tissue/organ being caused by a microbial, chemical or physical agent. The Pathogenesis of a disease is the mechanism by which an etiological factor causes the disease. The term can also be used to describe the development of the disease, such as acute, chronic and recurrent.
Carcinoma	A Carcinoma is any malignant cancer that arises from epithelial cells. Carcinoma s invade surrounding tissues and organs and may metastasize, or spread, to lymph nodes and other sites.
Hypertrophy	Hypertrophy is the increase in the volume of an organ or tissue due to the enlargement of its component cells. It should be distinguished from hyperplasia, in which the cells remain approximately the same size but increase in number. Although Hypertrophy and hyperplasia are two distinct process, they frequently occur together, such as in the case of the hormonally-induced proliferation and enlargement of the cells of the uterus during pregnancy.
Idiopathic	Idiopathic is an adjective used primarily in medicine meaning arising spontaneously or from an obscure or unknown cause. From Greek á¼´διος, idios + πῐ¬θος, pathos (suffering), it means approximately "a disease of its own kind." It is technically a term from nosology, the classification of disease. For most medical conditions, one or more causes are somewhat understood, but in a certain percentage of people with the condition, the cause may not be readily apparent or characterized.
Diagnosis	In medicine, diagnosis is the process of identifying a medical condition or disease by its signs, symptoms, and from the results of various diagnostic procedures. The conclusion reached through this process is called a diagnosis. The term "diagnostic criteria" designates the combination of signs, symptoms, and test results that allows the doctor to ascertain the diagnosis of the respective disease.
Stenosis	A Stenosis is an abnormal narrowing in a blood vessel or other tubular organ or structure. It is also sometimes called a "stricture" (as in urethral stricture.)

The term "coarctation" is synonymous, but is commonly used only in the context of aortic coarctation.

Stroke

A Stroke is the rapidly developing loss of brain function(s) due to disturbance in the blood supply to the brain. This can be due to ischemia (lack of blood supply) caused by thrombosis or embolism or due to a hemorrhage. As a result, the affected area of the brain is unable to function, leading to inability to move one or more limbs on one side of the body, inability to understand or formulate speech, or inability to see one side of the visual field.

Neoplasm

Neoplasm is an abnormal mass of tissue as a result of neoplasia. Neoplasia is the abnormal proliferation of cells. The growth of this clone of cells exceeds, and is uncoordinated with, that of the normal tissues around it.

Endotoxin

Endotoxin s (not to be confused with enterotoxin) are toxins associated with certain bacteria. Classically, an Endotoxin is a toxin that, unlike an "exotoxin", is not secreted in soluble form by live bacteria, but is a structural component in the bacteria which is released mainly when bacteria are lysed. Structure of a lipopolysaccharide

The prototypical examples of Endotoxin are lipopolysaccharide (LPS) or lipo-oligo-saccharide (LOS) found in the outer membrane of various Gram-negative bacteria and is an important cause of their ability to cause disease.

Inflammation

Inflammation is the complex biological response of vascular tissues to harmful stimuli, such as pathogens, damaged cells, or irritants. It is a protective attempt by the organism to remove the injurious stimuli as well as initiate the healing process for the tissue. Inflammation is not a synonym for infection.

Etiology	Etiology is the study of causation, or origination.
	The word is most commonly used in medical and philosophical theories, where it is used to refer to the study of why things occur, or even the reasons behind the way that things act, and is used in philosophy, physics, psychology, government, medicine, theology and biology in reference to the causes of various phenomena. An etiological myth is a myth intended to explain a name or create a mythic history for a place or family.
Pathophysiology	Pathophysiology is the study of the changes of normal mechanical, physical, and biochemical functions, either caused by a disease, or resulting from an abnormal syndrome. More formally, it is the branch of medicine which deals with any disturbances of body functions, caused by disease or prodromal symptoms.
	An alternate definition is "the study of the biological and physical manifestations of disease as they correlate with the underlying abnormalities and physiological disturbances."
	The study of pathology and the study of Pathophysiology often involves substantial overlap in diseases and processes, but pathology emphasizes direct observations, while Pathophysiology emphasizes quantifiable measurements.
Stenosis	A Stenosis is an abnormal narrowing in a blood vessel or other tubular organ or structure.
	It is also sometimes called a "stricture" (as in urethral stricture.)
	The term "coarctation" is synonymous, but is commonly used only in the context of aortic coarctation.
Merozoite surface protein	A Merozoite surface protein is a protein molecule taken from the skin of a merozoite. A merozoite is a "daughter cell" of a protozoan.
	Merozoite surface protein s are useful in researching malaria, a disease caused by protozoans.
Blood test	A Blood test is a laboratory analysis performed on a blood sample that is usually extracted from a vein in the arm using a needle, or via fingerprick.
	Blood test s are used to determine physiological and biochemical states, such as disease, mineral content, drug effectiveness, and organ function. Although the term Blood test is used, most routine tests (except for most haematology) are done on plasma or serum, instead of blood cells.

Glaucoma	Glaucoma refers to a group of diseases that affect the optic nerve and involves a loss of retinal ganglion cells in a characteristic pattern. It is a type of optic neuropathy. Raised intraocular pressure is a significant risk factor for developing Glaucoma
Merozoite surface protein	A Merozoite surface protein is a protein molecule taken from the skin of a merozoite. A merozoite is a "daughter cell" of a protozoan. Merozoite surface protein s are useful in researching malaria, a disease caused by protozoans.
Leukemia	Leukemia is a cancer of the blood or bone marrow and is characterized by an abnormal proliferation (production by multiplication) of blood cells, usually white blood cells (leukocytes.) Leukemia is a broad term covering a spectrum of diseases. In turn, it is part of the even broader group of diseases called haematological neoplasms.
Total iron-binding capacity	Total iron-binding capacity is a medical laboratory test which measures the blood"s capacity to bind iron with transferrin. It is performed by drawing blood and measuring the maximum amount of iron that it can carry, which indirectly measures transferrin since transferrin is the most dynamic carrier. TIBC is less expensive than a direct measurement of transferrin.

Cavitation	Cavitation is the formation of vapour bubbles of a flowing liquid in a region where the pressure of the liquid falls below its vapor pressure. Cavitation is usually divided into two classes of behavior: inertial (or transient) Cavitation and noninertial Cavitation Inertial Cavitation is the process where a void or bubble in a liquid rapidly collapses, producing a shock wave.
Pathogenesis	The term Pathogenesis means step by step development of a disease and the chain of events leading to that disease due to a series of changes in the structure and /or function of a cell/tissue/organ being caused by a microbial, chemical or physical agent. The Pathogenesis of a disease is the mechanism by which an etiological factor causes the disease. The term can also be used to describe the development of the disease, such as acute, chronic and recurrent.
Pathophysiology	Pathophysiology is the study of the changes of normal mechanical, physical, and biochemical functions, either caused by a disease, or resulting from an abnormal syndrome. More formally, it is the branch of medicine which deals with any disturbances of body functions, caused by disease or prodromal symptoms. An alternate definition is "the study of the biological and physical manifestations of disease as they correlate with the underlying abnormalities and physiological disturbances." The study of pathology and the study of Pathophysiology often involves substantial overlap in diseases and processes, but pathology emphasizes direct observations, while Pathophysiology emphasizes quantifiable measurements.
Cancer	Cancer is a class of diseases in which a group of cells display uncontrolled growth (division beyond the normal limits), invasion (intrusion on and destruction of adjacent tissues), and sometimes metastasis (spread to other locations in the body via lymph or blood.) These three malignant properties of cancers differentiate them from benign tumors, which are self-limited, and do not invade or metastasize. Most cancers form a tumor but some, like leukemia, do not.
Primary	In medicine, the reporting of symptoms by a patient may have significant psychological motivators. Psychologists sometimes categorize these motivators into primary or secondary gain. primary gain is internally good; motivationally.
Carcinoma	A Carcinoma is any malignant cancer that arises from epithelial cells. Carcinoma s invade surrounding tissues and organs and may metastasize, or spread, to lymph nodes and other sites.
Mucoepidermoid carcinoma	Mucoepidermoid carcinoma is the most common type of salivary gland malignancy in children. Mucoepidermoid carcinoma can also be found in other organs. It has been rarely reported in the lacrimal sac and thyroid as well as other more common locations.
Fibroepithelial neoplasms	Fibroepithelial neoplasms are biphasic tumors. This means they consist of epithelial tissue, and stromal or mesenchymal tissue. They may be benign or malignant.

Pathophysiology	Pathophysiology is the study of the changes of normal mechanical, physical, and biochemical functions, either caused by a disease, or resulting from an abnormal syndrome. More formally, it is the branch of medicine which deals with any disturbances of body functions, caused by disease or prodromal symptoms.
	An alternate definition is "the study of the biological and physical manifestations of disease as they correlate with the underlying abnormalities and physiological disturbances."
	The study of pathology and the study of Pathophysiology often involves substantial overlap in diseases and processes, but pathology emphasizes direct observations, while Pathophysiology emphasizes quantifiable measurements.
Cancer	Cancer is a class of diseases in which a group of cells display uncontrolled growth (division beyond the normal limits), invasion (intrusion on and destruction of adjacent tissues), and sometimes metastasis (spread to other locations in the body via lymph or blood.) These three malignant properties of cancers differentiate them from benign tumors, which are self-limited, and do not invade or metastasize. Most cancers form a tumor but some, like leukemia, do not.
Subglottic stenosis	Subglottic stenosis is a congenital or acquired narrowing of the subglottic airway. Although it is relatively rare, it is the third most common congenital airway problem (after laryngomalacia and vocal cord paralysis.) Subglottic stenosis can present as a life-threatening airway emergency.
Dysplasia	Dysplasia is a term used in pathology to refer to an abnormality in maturation of cells within a tissue. This generally consists of an expansion of immature cells, with a corresponding decrease in the number and location of mature cells. Dysplasia is often indicative of an early neoplastic process.
Pathogenesis	The term Pathogenesis means step by step development of a disease and the chain of events leading to that disease due to a series of changes in the structure and /or function of a cell/tissue/organ being caused by a microbial, chemical or physical agent. The Pathogenesis of a disease is the mechanism by which an etiological factor causes the disease. The term can also be used to describe the development of the disease, such as acute, chronic and recurrent.
Bilirubin	Bilirubin is the yellow breakdown product of normal heme catabolism. Heme is found in hemoglobin, a principal component of red blood cells. Bilirubin is excreted in bile, and its levels are elevated in certain diseases.
Blood test	A Blood test is a laboratory analysis performed on a blood sample that is usually extracted from a vein in the arm using a needle, or via fingerprick.
	Blood test s are used to determine physiological and biochemical states, such as disease, mineral content, drug effectiveness, and organ function. Although the term Blood test is used, most routine tests (except for most haematology) are done on plasma or serum, instead of blood cells.

Fibroepithelial neoplasms	Fibroepithelial neoplasms are biphasic tumors. This means they consist of epithelial tissue, and stromal or mesenchymal tissue. They may be benign or malignant.
Blood test	A Blood test is a laboratory analysis performed on a blood sample that is usually extracted from a vein in the arm using a needle, or via fingerprick. Blood test s are used to determine physiological and biochemical states, such as disease, mineral content, drug effectiveness, and organ function. Although the term Blood test is used, most routine tests (except for most haematology) are done on plasma or serum, instead of blood cells.
Blood urea nitrogen	The Blood urea nitrogen test is a measure of the amount of nitrogen in the blood in the form of urea, and a measurement of renal function. Urea is a substance secreted by the liver, and removed from the blood by the kidneys. The liver produces urea in the urea cycle as a waste product of the digestion of protein.
Gingivitis	Gingivitis around the teeth is a general term for gingival diseases affecting the gingiva As generally used, the term Gingivitis refers to gingival inflammation induced by bacterial biofilms adherent to tooth surfaces. Gingivitis can be defined as inflammation of the gingival tissue without loss of tooth attachment

Pathophysiology	Pathophysiology is the study of the changes of normal mechanical, physical, and biochemical functions, either caused by a disease, or resulting from an abnormal syndrome. More formally, it is the branch of medicine which deals with any disturbances of body functions, caused by disease or prodromal symptoms.
	An alternate definition is "the study of the biological and physical manifestations of disease as they correlate with the underlying abnormalities and physiological disturbances."
	The study of pathology and the study of Pathophysiology often involves substantial overlap in diseases and processes, but pathology emphasizes direct observations, while Pathophysiology emphasizes quantifiable measurements.
Dysplasia	Dysplasia is a term used in pathology to refer to an abnormality in maturation of cells within a tissue. This generally consists of an expansion of immature cells, with a corresponding decrease in the number and location of mature cells. Dysplasia is often indicative of an early neoplastic process.
Hypertrophy	Hypertrophy is the increase in the volume of an organ or tissue due to the enlargement of its component cells. It should be distinguished from hyperplasia, in which the cells remain approximately the same size but increase in number. Although Hypertrophy and hyperplasia are two distinct process, they frequently occur together, such as in the case of the hormonally-induced proliferation and enlargement of the cells of the uterus during pregnancy.
Idiopathic	Idiopathic is an adjective used primarily in medicine meaning arising spontaneously or from an obscure or unknown cause. From Greek á¼΄διος, idios + πΐ¬θος, pathos (suffering), it means approximately "a disease of its own kind."
	It is technically a term from nosology, the classification of disease. For most medical conditions, one or more causes are somewhat understood, but in a certain percentage of people with the condition, the cause may not be readily apparent or characterized.
Fibroepithelial neoplasms	Fibroepithelial neoplasms are biphasic tumors. This means they consist of epithelial tissue, and stromal or mesenchymal tissue. They may be benign or malignant.
Adenoma	An Adenoma is a benign tumor (-oma) of glandular origin. Adenoma s can grow from many organs including the colon, adrenal glands, pituitary gland, thyroid, etc. Although these growths are benign, over time they may progress to become malignant, at which point they are called adenocarcinomas.
Carcinoma	A Carcinoma is any malignant cancer that arises from epithelial cells. Carcinoma s invade surrounding tissues and organs and may metastasize, or spread, to lymph nodes and other sites.
Inflammation	Inflammation is the complex biological response of vascular tissues to harmful stimuli, such as pathogens, damaged cells, or irritants. It is a protective attempt by the organism to remove the injurious stimuli as well as initiate the healing process for the tissue. Inflammation is not a synonym for infection.

Pathogenesis	The term Pathogenesis means step by step development of a disease and the chain of events leading to that disease due to a series of changes in the structure and /or function of a cell/tissue/organ being caused by a microbial, chemical or physical agent. The Pathogenesis of a disease is the mechanism by which an etiological factor causes the disease. The term can also be used to describe the development of the disease, such as acute, chronic and recurrent.
Lesion	A Lesion is any abnormal tissue found on or in an organism, usually damaged by disease or trauma. Lesion is derived from the Latin word laesio which means injury. Lesion s are caused by any process that damages tissues.
Electrolyte	An Electrolyte is any substance containing free ions that behaves as an electrically conductive medium. Because they generally consist of ions in solution, Electrolyte s are also known as ionic solutions, but molten Electrolyte s and solid Electrolyte s are also possible. Electrolyte s commonly exist as solutions of acids, bases or salts.
Blood test	A Blood test is a laboratory analysis performed on a blood sample that is usually extracted from a vein in the arm using a needle, or via fingerprick. Blood test s are used to determine physiological and biochemical states, such as disease, mineral content, drug effectiveness, and organ function. Although the term Blood test is used, most routine tests (except for most haematology) are done on plasma or serum, instead of blood cells.
Cancer	Cancer is a class of diseases in which a group of cells display uncontrolled growth (division beyond the normal limits), invasion (intrusion on and destruction of adjacent tissues), and sometimes metastasis (spread to other locations in the body via lymph or blood.) These three malignant properties of cancers differentiate them from benign tumors, which are self-limited, and do not invade or metastasize. Most cancers form a tumor but some, like leukemia, do not.
Diagnosis	In medicine, diagnosis is the process of identifying a medical condition or disease by its signs, symptoms, and from the results of various diagnostic procedures. The conclusion reached through this process is called a diagnosis. The term "diagnostic criteria" designates the combination of signs, symptoms, and test results that allows the doctor to ascertain the diagnosis of the respective disease.

Electrolyte	An Electrolyte is any substance containing free ions that behaves as an electrically conductive medium. Because they generally consist of ions in solution, Electrolyte s are also known as ionic solutions, but molten Electrolyte s and solid Electrolyte s are also possible.
	Electrolyte s commonly exist as solutions of acids, bases or salts.
Dysplasia	Dysplasia is a term used in pathology to refer to an abnormality in maturation of cells within a tissue. This generally consists of an expansion of immature cells, with a corresponding decrease in the number and location of mature cells. Dysplasia is often indicative of an early neoplastic process.
Lesion	A Lesion is any abnormal tissue found on or in an organism, usually damaged by disease or trauma. Lesion is derived from the Latin word laesio which means injury.
	Lesion s are caused by any process that damages tissues.
Primary	In medicine, the reporting of symptoms by a patient may have significant psychological motivators. Psychologists sometimes categorize these motivators into primary or secondary gain.
	primary gain is internally good; motivationally.
Pathophysiology	Pathophysiology is the study of the changes of normal mechanical, physical, and biochemical functions, either caused by a disease, or resulting from an abnormal syndrome. More formally, it is the branch of medicine which deals with any disturbances of body functions, caused by disease or prodromal symptoms.
	An alternate definition is "the study of the biological and physical manifestations of disease as they correlate with the underlying abnormalities and physiological disturbances."
	The study of pathology and the study of Pathophysiology often involves substantial overlap in diseases and processes, but pathology emphasizes direct observations, while Pathophysiology emphasizes quantifiable measurements.
Neoplasm	Neoplasm is an abnormal mass of tissue as a result of neoplasia. Neoplasia is the abnormal proliferation of cells. The growth of this clone of cells exceeds, and is uncoordinated with, that of the normal tissues around it.
Pathogenesis	The term Pathogenesis means step by step development of a disease and the chain of events leading to that disease due to a series of changes in the structure and /or function of a cell/tissue/organ being caused by a microbial, chemical or physical agent. The Pathogenesis of a disease is the mechanism by which an etiological factor causes the disease. The term can also be used to describe the development of the disease, such as acute, chronic and recurrent.

Hypertrophy	Hypertrophy is the increase in the volume of an organ or tissue due to the enlargement of its component cells. It should be distinguished from hyperplasia, in which the cells remain approximately the same size but increase in number. Although Hypertrophy and hyperplasia are two distinct process, they frequently occur together, such as in the case of the hormonally-induced proliferation and enlargement of the cells of the uterus during pregnancy.
Primary	In medicine, the reporting of symptoms by a patient may have significant psychological motivators. Psychologists sometimes categorize these motivators into primary or secondary gain. primary gain is internally good; motivationally.
Pathophysiology	Pathophysiology is the study of the changes of normal mechanical, physical, and biochemical functions, either caused by a disease, or resulting from an abnormal syndrome. More formally, it is the branch of medicine which deals with any disturbances of body functions, caused by disease or prodromal symptoms. An alternate definition is "the study of the biological and physical manifestations of disease as they correlate with the underlying abnormalities and physiological disturbances." The study of pathology and the study of Pathophysiology often involves substantial overlap in diseases and processes, but pathology emphasizes direct observations, while Pathophysiology emphasizes quantifiable measurements.
Glucose	Glucose, a monosaccharide also known as grape sugar, blood sugar is a very important carbohydrate in biology. The living cell uses it as a source of energy and metabolic intermediate. Glucose is one of the main products of photosynthesis and starts cellular respiration in both prokaryotes and eukaryotes
Cancer	Cancer is a class of diseases in which a group of cells display uncontrolled growth (division beyond the normal limits), invasion (intrusion on and destruction of adjacent tissues), and sometimes metastasis (spread to other locations in the body via lymph or blood.) These three malignant properties of cancers differentiate them from benign tumors, which are self-limited, and do not invade or metastasize. Most cancers form a tumor but some, like leukemia, do not.
Transferrin	Transferrin is a blood plasma protein for iron ion delivery that, in humans, is encoded by the TF gene. Transferrin is a glycoprotein that binds iron very tightly but reversibly. Although iron bound to Transferrin is less than 0.1% (4 mg) of the total body iron, it is the most important iron pool, with the highest rate of turnover (25 mg/24 h.)
Inflammation	Inflammation is the complex biological response of vascular tissues to harmful stimuli, such as pathogens, damaged cells, or irritants. It is a protective attempt by the organism to remove the injurious stimuli as well as initiate the healing process for the tissue. Inflammation is not a synonym for infection.

Liver function tests	Liver function tests, which include liver enzymes, are groups of clinical biochemistry laboratory blood assays designed to give information about the state of a patient"s liver. Most liver diseases cause only mild symptoms initially, but it is vital that these diseases be detected early. Hepatic (liver) involvement in some diseases can be of crucial importance.
Bilirubin	Bilirubin is the yellow breakdown product of normal heme catabolism. Heme is found in hemoglobin, a principal component of red blood cells. Bilirubin is excreted in bile, and its levels are elevated in certain diseases.

Pathophysiology	Pathophysiology is the study of the changes of normal mechanical, physical, and biochemical functions, either caused by a disease, or resulting from an abnormal syndrome. More formally, it is the branch of medicine which deals with any disturbances of body functions, caused by disease or prodromal symptoms. An alternate definition is "the study of the biological and physical manifestations of disease as they correlate with the underlying abnormalities and physiological disturbances." The study of pathology and the study of Pathophysiology often involves substantial overlap in diseases and processes, but pathology emphasizes direct observations, while Pathophysiology emphasizes quantifiable measurements.
Intracranial hemorrhage	An Intracranial hemorrhage is a hemorrhage within the skull. Intracranial bleeding occurs when a blood vessel within the skull is ruptured or leaks. It can result from physical trauma (as occurs in head injury) or nontraumatic causes (as occurs in hemorrhagic stroke) such as a ruptured aneurysm.
Esophagitis	Esophagitis is inflammation of the esophagus. · The most common cause is gastroesophageal reflux disease (GERD)(GORD in UK.) If caused by GERD, the diseases is also called reflux Esophagitis. · Other causes of Esophagitis include infections (most commonly candida, herpes simplex and cytomegalovirus.) These infections are typically seen in immunocompromised people, such as those with HIV. · Chemical injury by alkaline or acid solutions may also cause Esophagitis, and is usually seen in children or in adults who attempt suicide · Physical injury resulting from radiation therapy or by nasogastric tubes may also be responsible. · Eosinophilic Esophagitis is a little understood form of Esophagitis, which is thought to be related to food allergies. · hyper acidity .
Diagnosis	In medicine, diagnosis is the process of identifying a medical condition or disease by its signs, symptoms, and from the results of various diagnostic procedures. The conclusion reached through this process is called a diagnosis. The term "diagnostic criteria" designates the combination of signs, symptoms, and test results that allows the doctor to ascertain the diagnosis of the respective disease.
Neoplasm	Neoplasm is an abnormal mass of tissue as a result of neoplasia. Neoplasia is the abnormal proliferation of cells. The growth of this clone of cells exceeds, and is uncoordinated with, that of the normal tissues around it.
Cancer	Cancer is a class of diseases in which a group of cells display uncontrolled growth (division beyond the normal limits), invasion (intrusion on and destruction of adjacent tissues), and sometimes metastasis (spread to other locations in the body via lymph or blood.) These three malignant properties of cancers differentiate them from benign tumors, which are self-limited, and do not invade or metastasize. Most cancers form a tumor but some, like leukemia, do not.

Lesion	A Lesion is any abnormal tissue found on or in an organism, usually damaged by disease or trauma. Lesion is derived from the Latin word laesio which means injury. Lesion s are caused by any process that damages tissues.
Fibroepithelial neoplasms	Fibroepithelial neoplasms are biphasic tumors. This means they consist of epithelial tissue, and stromal or mesenchymal tissue. They may be benign or malignant.
Inflammation	Inflammation is the complex biological response of vascular tissues to harmful stimuli, such as pathogens, damaged cells, or irritants. It is a protective attempt by the organism to remove the injurious stimuli as well as initiate the healing process for the tissue. Inflammation is not a synonym for infection.
Alcoholic liver disease	Alcoholic liver disease is the major cause of liver disease in Western countries, (in Asian countries, viral hepatitis is the major cause.) It arises from the excessive ingestion of alcohol. Pathogenesis of alcohol induced liver injury Fatty change, or steatosis is the accumulation of fat in liver cells which can be seen as fatty globules under the microscope.
Carcinoma	A Carcinoma is any malignant cancer that arises from epithelial cells. Carcinoma s invade surrounding tissues and organs and may metastasize, or spread, to lymph nodes and other sites.
Pathogenesis	The term Pathogenesis means step by step development of a disease and the chain of events leading to that disease due to a series of changes in the structure and /or function of a cell/tissue/organ being caused by a microbial, chemical or physical agent. The Pathogenesis of a disease is the mechanism by which an etiological factor causes the disease. The term can also be used to describe the development of the disease, such as acute, chronic and recurrent.

Pathophysiology	Pathophysiology is the study of the changes of normal mechanical, physical, and biochemical functions, either caused by a disease, or resulting from an abnormal syndrome. More formally, it is the branch of medicine which deals with any disturbances of body functions, caused by disease or prodromal symptoms.
	An alternate definition is "the study of the biological and physical manifestations of disease as they correlate with the underlying abnormalities and physiological disturbances."
	The study of pathology and the study of Pathophysiology often involves substantial overlap in diseases and processes, but pathology emphasizes direct observations, while Pathophysiology emphasizes quantifiable measurements.
Stenosis	A Stenosis is an abnormal narrowing in a blood vessel or other tubular organ or structure.
	It is also sometimes called a "stricture" (as in urethral stricture.)
	The term "coarctation" is synonymous, but is commonly used only in the context of aortic coarctation.
Hyperplasia	Hyperplasia is a general term referring to the proliferation of cells within an organ or tissue beyond that which is ordinarily seen (e.g. constantly dividing cells.) Hyperplasia may result in the gross enlargement of an organ, the formation of a benign tumor, or may be visible only under a microscope. Hyperplasia is different from hypertrophy in that the adaptive cell change in hypertrophy is by increased cellular size only, whereas in Hyperplasia it is by increased cellular number.

Blood test	A Blood test is a laboratory analysis performed on a blood sample that is usually extracted from a vein in the arm using a needle, or via fingerprick.
	Blood test s are used to determine physiological and biochemical states, such as disease, mineral content, drug effectiveness, and organ function. Although the term Blood test is used, most routine tests (except for most haematology) are done on plasma or serum, instead of blood cells.
Toxoplasmosis	Toxoplasmosis is a parasitic disease caused by the protozoan Toxoplasma gondii. The parasite infects most genera of warm-blooded animals, including humans, but the primary host is the felid (cat) family. Animals are infected by eating infected meat, by ingestion of feces of a cat that has itself recently been infected, or by transmission from mother to fetus.
Creatine kinase	Creatine kinase is an enzyme expressed by various tissues and cell types. Creatine kinase catalyses the conversion of creatine and consumes adenosine triphosphate to create phosphocreatine and adenosine diphosphate This Creatine kinase enzyme reaction is reversible, such that also ATP can be generated from PCr and ADP.
	In tissues and cells that consume ATP rapidly, especially skeletal muscle, but also brain, photoreceptor cells of the retina, hair cells of the inner ear, spermatozoa and smooth muscle, phosphocreatine serves as an energy reservoir for the rapid buffering and regeneration of ATP in situ, as well as for intracellular energy transport by the phosphocreatine shuttle or circuit.

Pathophysiology

Pathophysiology is the study of the changes of normal mechanical, physical, and biochemical functions, either caused by a disease, or resulting from an abnormal syndrome. More formally, it is the branch of medicine which deals with any disturbances of body functions, caused by disease or prodromal symptoms.

An alternate definition is "the study of the biological and physical manifestations of disease as they correlate with the underlying abnormalities and physiological disturbances."

The study of pathology and the study of Pathophysiology often involves substantial overlap in diseases and processes, but pathology emphasizes direct observations, while Pathophysiology emphasizes quantifiable measurements.

Fixation

In the fields of histology, pathology, and cell biology, Fixation is a chemical process by which biological tissues are preserved from decay, either through autolysis or putrefaction. Fixation terminates any ongoing biochemical reactions, and may also increase the mechanical strength or stability of the treated tissues.

The purpose of Fixation is to preserve a sample of biological material (tissue or cells) as close to its natural state as possible in the process of preparing tissue for examination.

Lesion

A Lesion is any abnormal tissue found on or in an organism, usually damaged by disease or trauma. Lesion is derived from the Latin word laesio which means injury.

Lesion s are caused by any process that damages tissues.

Osteopenia

Osteopenia is a condition where bone mineral density is lower than normal. It is considered by many doctors to be a precursor to osteoporosis. However, not every person diagnosed with Osteopenia will develop osteoporosis.

Paclitaxel

Paclitaxel is a mitotic inhibitor used in cancer chemotherapy. It was discovered in a National Cancer Institute program at the Research Triangle Institute in 1967 when Monroe E. Wall and Mansukh C. Wani isolated it from the bark of the Pacific Yew tree, Taxus brevifolia and named it "taxol". When it was developed commercially by Bristol-Myers Squibb (BMS) the generic name was changed to "Paclitaxel" and the BMS compound is sold under the trademark "TAXOL".

Sequestrum

A Sequestrum is a piece of dead bone that has become separated during the process of necrosis from normal/sound bone.

It is a complication (sequela) of osteomyelitis. The pathological process is as follows:

· infection in the bone leads to an increase in intramedullary pressure due to inflammatory exudates
· the periosteum becomes stripped from the osteum, leading to vascular thrombosis
· bone necrosis follows due to lack of blood supply
· sequestra are formed An X-ray of a child"s femur showing a bony Sequestrum highlighted by the blue arrow.

The sequestra are surrounded by sclerotic bone which is relatively avascular (without a blood supply.) Within the bone itself, the haversian canals become blocked with scar tissue, and the bone becomes surrounded by thickened periosteum.

Fibroepithelial neoplasms	Fibroepithelial neoplasms are biphasic tumors. This means they consist of epithelial tissue, and stromal or mesenchymal tissue. They may be benign or malignant.
Diagnosis	In medicine, diagnosis is the process of identifying a medical condition or disease by its signs, symptoms, and from the results of various diagnostic procedures. The conclusion reached through this process is called a diagnosis. The term "diagnostic criteria" designates the combination of signs, symptoms, and test results that allows the doctor to ascertain the diagnosis of the respective disease.
Cancer	Cancer is a class of diseases in which a group of cells display uncontrolled growth (division beyond the normal limits), invasion (intrusion on and destruction of adjacent tissues), and sometimes metastasis (spread to other locations in the body via lymph or blood.) These three malignant properties of cancers differentiate them from benign tumors, which are self-limited, and do not invade or metastasize. Most cancers form a tumor but some, like leukemia, do not.
Sarcoma	A Sarcoma is a cancer of the connective tissue resulting in mesoderm proliferation. This is in contrast to carcinomas, which are of epithelial origin (breast, colon, pancreas, and others.) However, due to an evolving understanding of tissue origin, the term "Sarcoma" is sometimes applied to tumors now known to arise from epithelial tissue.
Rheumatoid nodule	A Rheumatoid nodule is a local swelling or tissue lump, usually rather firm to touch, like an unripe fruit, which occurs almost exclusively in association with rheumatoid arthritis. Very rarely Rheumatoid nodules occur as "rheumatoid nodulosis" in the absence of arthritis. They are usually subcutaneous especially over bony prominences such as the tip of the elbow or olecranon or over the finger knuckles.
Primary	In medicine, the reporting of symptoms by a patient may have significant psychological motivators. Psychologists sometimes categorize these motivators into primary or secondary gain. primary gain is internally good; motivationally.
Atrophy	Atrophy is the partial or complete wasting away of a part of the body. Causes of Atrophy include poor nourishment, poor circulation, loss of hormonal support, loss of nerve supply to the target organ, disuse or lack of exercise or disease intrinsic to the tissue itself. Hormonal and nerve inputs that maintain an organ or body part are referred to as trophic.
Trichinella	Trichinella is the genus of parasitic roundworms of the phylum Nematoda that cause trichinosis. Members of this genus are often called Trichinella or trichina worms. A characteristic of nematoda are one-way digestive tract, and a pseudoceolom (body cavity made up of only an ectoderm and endoderm.)
Rhabdomyosarcoma	A Rhabdomyosarcoma is a type of cancer, specifically a sarcoma (cancer of connective tissues), in which the cancer cells are thought to arise from skeletal muscle progenitors. It can also be found attached to muscle tissue, wrapped around intestines, or anywhere, to exclude the neck area.

Its two most common forms are embryonal Rhabdomyosarcoma and alveolar Rhabdomyosarcoma.

Primary	In medicine, the reporting of symptoms by a patient may have significant psychological motivators. Psychologists sometimes categorize these motivators into primary or secondary gain. primary gain is internally good; motivationally.
Dysplasia	Dysplasia is a term used in pathology to refer to an abnormality in maturation of cells within a tissue. This generally consists of an expansion of immature cells, with a corresponding decrease in the number and location of mature cells. Dysplasia is often indicative of an early neoplastic process.
Idiopathic	Idiopathic is an adjective used primarily in medicine meaning arising spontaneously or from an obscure or unknown cause. From Greek á¼´διος, idios + πÎ¬θος, pathos (suffering), it means approximately "a disease of its own kind." It is technically a term from nosology, the classification of disease. For most medical conditions, one or more causes are somewhat understood, but in a certain percentage of people with the condition, the cause may not be readily apparent or characterized.
Pathophysiology	Pathophysiology is the study of the changes of normal mechanical, physical, and biochemical functions, either caused by a disease, or resulting from an abnormal syndrome. More formally, it is the branch of medicine which deals with any disturbances of body functions, caused by disease or prodromal symptoms. An alternate definition is "the study of the biological and physical manifestations of disease as they correlate with the underlying abnormalities and physiological disturbances." The study of pathology and the study of Pathophysiology often involves substantial overlap in diseases and processes, but pathology emphasizes direct observations, while Pathophysiology emphasizes quantifiable measurements.
Diagnosis	In medicine, diagnosis is the process of identifying a medical condition or disease by its signs, symptoms, and from the results of various diagnostic procedures. The conclusion reached through this process is called a diagnosis. The term "diagnostic criteria" designates the combination of signs, symptoms, and test results that allows the doctor to ascertain the diagnosis of the respective disease.
Aneurysm	An Aneurysm (or aneurism) is a localized, blood-filled dilation of a blood vessel caused by disease or weakening of the vessel wall. Aneurysm s most commonly occur in arteries at the base of the brain (the circle of Willis) and in the aorta (the main artery coming out of the heart, a so-called aortic Aneurysm) As the size of an Aneurysm increases, there is an increased risk of rupture, which can result in severe hemorrhage or other complications including sudden death.
Bone cyst	A Bone cyst is a type of cyst that can present in the jaw, or on other locations in the body. Types include:

.

| | | · Aneurysmal Bone cyst
· Traumatic Bone cyst |

Acquired
Alignment

Chondropathies
Both

Osteoid osteoma	An Osteoid osteoma is a benign tumor which arises from osteoblasts and originally thought to be a smaller version of an osteoblastoma. Characterized by less than 1.5cm diameter, Osteoid osteoma s most frequently occur in young men in the vertebrae or in the long bones and less commonly in the mandible or other craniofacial bones. Severe pain typically occurs at night.
Fibroepithelial neoplasms	Fibroepithelial neoplasms are biphasic tumors. This means they consist of epithelial tissue, and stromal or mesenchymal tissue. They may be benign or malignant.
Sarcoma	A Sarcoma is a cancer of the connective tissue resulting in mesoderm proliferation. This is in contrast to carcinomas, which are of epithelial origin (breast, colon, pancreas, and others.) However, due to an evolving understanding of tissue origin, the term "Sarcoma" is sometimes applied to tumors now known to arise from epithelial tissue.
Rhabdomyosarcoma	A Rhabdomyosarcoma is a type of cancer, specifically a sarcoma (cancer of connective tissues), in which the cancer cells are thought to arise from skeletal muscle progenitors. It can also be found attached to muscle tissue, wrapped around intestines, or anywhere, to exclude the neck area. Its two most common forms are embryonal Rhabdomyosarcoma and alveolar Rhabdomyosarcoma.

Atrophy	Atrophy is the partial or complete wasting away of a part of the body. Causes of Atrophy include poor nourishment, poor circulation, loss of hormonal support, loss of nerve supply to the target organ, disuse or lack of exercise or disease intrinsic to the tissue itself. Hormonal and nerve inputs that maintain an organ or body part are referred to as trophic.
Lesion	A Lesion is any abnormal tissue found on or in an organism, usually damaged by disease or trauma. Lesion is derived from the Latin word laesio which means injury. Lesion s are caused by any process that damages tissues.
Fibroepithelial neoplasms	Fibroepithelial neoplasms are biphasic tumors. This means they consist of epithelial tissue, and stromal or mesenchymal tissue. They may be benign or malignant.
Cancer	Cancer is a class of diseases in which a group of cells display uncontrolled growth (division beyond the normal limits), invasion (intrusion on and destruction of adjacent tissues), and sometimes metastasis (spread to other locations in the body via lymph or blood.) These three malignant properties of cancers differentiate them from benign tumors, which are self-limited, and do not invade or metastasize. Most cancers form a tumor but some, like leukemia, do not.
Squamous cell carcinoma	In medicine, Squamous cell carcinoma is a form of cancer of the carcinoma type that may occur in many different organs, including the skin, lips, mouth, esophagus, urinary bladder, prostate, lungs, vagina, and cervix. It is a malignant tumor of squamous epithelium (epithelium that shows squamous cell differentiation.)
	Squamous cell carcinoma may be classified into the following types:[473]
	· Adenoid Squamous cell carcinoma · Clear cell Squamous cell carcinoma (Clear cell carcinoma of the skin) · Spindle cell Squamous cell carcinoma · Signet-ring cell Squamous cell carcinoma · Basaloid Squamous cell carcinoma · Verrucous carcinoma · Keratoacanthoma
	A large Squamous cell carcinoma of the tongue.
	A carcinoma can be characterized as either in situ (confined to the original site) or invasive, depending on whether the cancer invades underlying tissues; only invasive cancers are able to spread to other organs and cause metastasis. Squamous cell carcinoma in situ are also called Bowen"s disease.
Toxoplasmosis	Toxoplasmosis is a parasitic disease caused by the protozoan Toxoplasma gondii. The parasite infects most genera of warm-blooded animals, including humans, but the primary host is the felid (cat) family. Animals are infected by eating infected meat, by ingestion of feces of a cat that has itself recently been infected, or by transmission from mother to fetus.

Lichen planus	Lichen planus is a chronic mucocutaneous disease that affects the skin and the oral mucosa, and presents itself in the form of papules, lesions or rashes. Lichen planus does not involve lichens; the name refers to the appearance of affected skin. Lichen planus may be divided into the following types:[466] · Configuration · Annular Lichen planus · Linear Lichen planus · Morphology of lesion · Hypertrophic Lichen planus · Atrophic Lichen planus · Vesiculobullous Lichen planus · Ulcerative Lichen planus · Follicular Lichen planus · Actinic Lichen planus · Lichen planus pigmentosus · Site of involvement · Lichen planus of the of the palms and soles (Palmoplantar Lichen planus) · Mucosal Lichen planus · Lichen planus of the nails · Lichen planus of the scalp · Inverse Lichen planus · Special forms

· Drug-induced Lichen planus
· Lupus erythematosus-Lichen planus overlap syndrome
· Lichen planus pemphigoides
· Keratosis lichenoides chronica
· Lichenoid reaction of graft-versus-host disease
· Lichenoid keratosis
· Lichenoid dermatitis

The cause of Lichen planus is not known. It is not contagious and does not involve any known pathogen.

Pemphigus	Pemphigus is a rare group of autoimmune blistering diseases that affect the skin and mucous membranes.
	In Pemphigus, autoantibodies form against desmoglein. Desmoglein forms the "glue" that attaches adjacent epidermal cells via attachment points called desmosomes.
Carbuncle	A Carbuncle is an abscess larger than a boil, usually with one or more openings draining pus onto the skin. It is usually caused by bacterial infection, most commonly Staphylococcus aureus. The infection is contagious and may spread to other areas of the body or other people.
Mosquito	Mosquito is a common insect in the family Culicidae .
	Mosquito es go through four stages in their life cycle: egg, larva, pupa, and adult or imago. The adult females lay their eggs in water, which can be a salt-marsh, a lake, a puddle, a natural reservoir on a plant, or an artificial water container such as a plastic bucket.
Basal cell carcinoma	Basal cell carcinoma is the most common type of skin cancer. It rarely metastasizes or kills, but it is still considered malignant because it can cause significant destruction and disfigurement by invading surrounding tissues. Statistically, approximately 3 out of 10 Caucasians develop a basal cell cancer within their lifetime.
Carcinoma	A Carcinoma is any malignant cancer that arises from epithelial cells. Carcinoma s invade surrounding tissues and organs and may metastasize, or spread, to lymph nodes and other sites.
Nevus	Nevus is the medical term for sharply-circumscribed and chronic lesions of the skin. These lesions are commonly named birthmarks and moles. By definition, nevi are benign.
Sarcoma	A Sarcoma is a cancer of the connective tissue resulting in mesoderm proliferation.
	This is in contrast to carcinomas, which are of epithelial origin (breast, colon, pancreas, and others.) However, due to an evolving understanding of tissue origin, the term "Sarcoma" is sometimes applied to tumors now known to arise from epithelial tissue.

Toxin	A Toxin is a poisonous substance produced by living cells or organisms.
	For a toxic substance not produced by living organisms, "toxicant" is the more appropriate term, and "toxics" is an acceptable plural.
	Toxin s can be small molecules, peptides, or proteins that are capable of causing disease on contact with or absorption by body tissues interacting with biological macromolecules such as enzymes or cellular receptors.
Microsporum	Species of the fungus Microsporum form both macro- and microconidia on short conidiophores. Macroconidia are hyaline, multiseptate, variable in form, fusiform, spindle-shaped to obovate, ranging from 7 to 20 by 30 to 160 um in size, with thin- or thick-echinulate to verrucose cell walls. Their shape, size and cell wall features are important characteristics for species identification.
Mumps	Mumps or epidemic parotitis is a viral disease of the human species, caused by the Mumps virus. Prior to the development of vaccination and the introduction of a vaccine, it was a common childhood disease worldwide, and is still a significant threat to health in the third world.
	Painful swelling of the salivary glands (classically the parotid gland) is the most typical presentation.
Bedbug	The Bedbug (or bed bug) is an insect of the family Cimicidae that lives by hematophagy - feeding on the blood of humans and other warm-blooded hosts. Its name comes from its preferred habitat: mattresses, sofas, and other furniture. Although not strictly nocturnal, Bedbug s are mainly active at night.
Lice	Lice, are an order of over 3,000 species of wingless insects; three of which are classified as human disease agents. They are obligate ectoparasites of every avian and most mammalian orders. They are not found on Monotremes and a few eutherian orders, namely the bats, whales, dolphins and porpoises and pangolins
Pediculosis	Pediculosis is an infestation of lice -- blood-feeding ectoparasitic insects of the order Phthiraptera. The condition can occur in almost any species of warm-blooded animal (i.e., mammals and birds), including humans. Although "Pediculosis" in humans may properly refer to lice infestation of any part of the body, the term is sometimes used loosely to refer to Pediculosis capitis, the infestation of the human head with the specific head louse.
Nevus	Nevus is the medical term for sharply-circumscribed and chronic lesions of the skin. These lesions are commonly named birthmarks and moles. By definition, nevi are benign.

Glucose	Glucose, a monosaccharide also known as grape sugar, blood sugar is a very important carbohydrate in biology. The living cell uses it as a source of energy and metabolic intermediate. Glucose is one of the main products of photosynthesis and starts cellular respiration in both prokaryotes and eukaryotes
Seizure	An epileptic Seizure is a transient symptom of excessive or synchronous neuronal activity in the brain. It can manifest as an alteration in mental state, tonic or clonic movements, convulsions, and various other psychic symptoms (such as déjà vu or jamais vu.) The medical syndrome of recurrent, unprovoked Seizure s is termed epilepsy, but Seizure s can occur in people who do not have epilepsy.
Pathology	Pathology is the study and diagnosis of disease through examination of organs, tissues, bodily fluids, and whole bodies (autopsies.) The term also encompasses the related scientific study of disease processes, called General Pathology Medical Pathology is divided in two main branches, Anatomical Pathology and Clinical Pathology
Pathogenesis	The term Pathogenesis means step by step development of a disease and the chain of events leading to that disease due to a series of changes in the structure and /or function of a cell/tissue/organ being caused by a microbial, chemical or physical agent. The Pathogenesis of a disease is the mechanism by which an etiological factor causes the disease. The term can also be used to describe the development of the disease, such as acute, chronic and recurrent.
Primary	In medicine, the reporting of symptoms by a patient may have significant psychological motivators. Psychologists sometimes categorize these motivators into primary or secondary gain. primary gain is internally good; motivationally.
Merozoite surface protein	A Merozoite surface protein is a protein molecule taken from the skin of a merozoite. A merozoite is a "daughter cell" of a protozoan. Merozoite surface protein s are useful in researching malaria, a disease caused by protozoans.
Bipolar disorder	Bipolar disorder manic depressive disorder or bipolar affective disorder, is a psychiatric diagnosis that describes a category of mood disorders defined by the presence of one or more episodes of abnormally elevated mood clinically referred to as mania or, if milder, hypomania. Individuals who experience manic episodes also commonly experience depressive episodes or symptoms, or mixed episodes in which features of both mania and depression are present at the same time. These episodes are usually separated by periods of "normal" mood, but in some individuals, depression and mania may rapidly alternate, known as rapid cycling.
Schizophrenia	Schizophrenia , from the Greek roots skhizein and phrÄ"n, phren- (φρÎ®ν, φρεν-; "mind") is a psychiatric diagnosis that describes a mental disorder characterized by abnormalities in the perception or expression of reality. Distortions in perception may affect all five senses, including sight, hearing, taste, smell and touch, but most commonly manifest as auditory hallucinations, paranoid or bizarre delusions, or disorganized speech and thinking with significant social or occupational dysfunction. Onset of symptoms typically occurs in young adulthood, with approximately 0.4-0.6% of the population affected.

Stroke	A Stroke is the rapidly developing loss of brain function(s) due to disturbance in the blood supply to the brain. This can be due to ischemia (lack of blood supply) caused by thrombosis or embolism or due to a hemorrhage. As a result, the affected area of the brain is unable to function, leading to inability to move one or more limbs on one side of the body, inability to understand or formulate speech, or inability to see one side of the visual field.
Fibroepithelial neoplasms	Fibroepithelial neoplasms are biphasic tumors. This means they consist of epithelial tissue, and stromal or mesenchymal tissue. They may be benign or malignant.
Cancer	Cancer is a class of diseases in which a group of cells display uncontrolled growth (division beyond the normal limits), invasion (intrusion on and destruction of adjacent tissues), and sometimes metastasis (spread to other locations in the body via lymph or blood.) These three malignant properties of cancers differentiate them from benign tumors, which are self-limited, and do not invade or metastasize. Most cancers form a tumor but some, like leukemia, do not.
Seizure	An epileptic Seizure is a transient symptom of excessive or synchronous neuronal activity in the brain. It can manifest as an alteration in mental state, tonic or clonic movements, convulsions, and various other psychic symptoms (such as déjà vu or jamais vu.) The medical syndrome of recurrent, unprovoked Seizure s is termed epilepsy, but Seizure s can occur in people who do not have epilepsy.
Schizophrenia	Schizophrenia , from the Greek roots skhizein and phrÄ"n, phren- (φρÎ®ν, φρεν-; "mind") is a psychiatric diagnosis that describes a mental disorder characterized by abnormalities in the perception or expression of reality. Distortions in perception may affect all five senses, including sight, hearing, taste, smell and touch, but most commonly manifest as auditory hallucinations, paranoid or bizarre delusions, or disorganized speech and thinking with significant social or occupational dysfunction. Onset of symptoms typically occurs in young adulthood, with approximately 0.4-0.6% of the population affected.

CPSIA information can be obtained at www.ICGtesting.com
Printed in the USA
245328LV00001B/28/P